Microaggressions and Traumatic Stress

Theory, Research, and Clinical Treatment

Kevin L. Nadal

AMERICAN PSYCHOLOGICAL ASSOCIATION
Washington, DC

Published by
American Psychological Association
750 First Street, NE
Washington, DC 20002
www.apa.org

APA Order Department
P.O. Box 92984
Washington, DC 20090-2984
Phone: (800) 374-2721; Direct: (202) 336-5510
Fax: (202) 336-5502; TDD/TTY: (202) 336-6123
Online: http://www.apa.org/pubs/books
E-mail: order@apa.org

In the U.K., Europe, Africa, and the Middle East, copies may be ordered from
Eurospan Group
c/o Turpin Distribution
Pegasus Drive
Stratton Business Park
Biggleswade Bedfordshire
SG18 8TQ United Kingdom
Phone: +44 (0) 1767 604972
Fax: +44 (0) 1767 601640
Online: https://www.eurospanbookstore.com/apa
E-mail: eurospan@turpin-distribution.com

Typeset in Minion by Circle Graphics, Inc., Columbia, MD

Printer: Edwards Brothers Malloy, Lillington, NC
Cover Designer: Mercury Publishing Services, Inc., Rockville, MD

Library of Congress Cataloging-in-Publication Data
Names: Nadal, Kevin L., author.
Title: Microaggressions and traumatic stress : theory, research, and clinical
    treatment / Kevin L. Nadal.
Description: First edition. | Washington, DC : American Psychological
    Association, 2018. | Series: Concise guides on trauma care book series |
    Includes bibliographical references and index.
Identifiers: LCCN 2017028787| ISBN 9781433828591 | ISBN 1433828596
Subjects: LCSH: Microaggressions. | Psychic trauma. | Stress (Psychology)

Classification: LCC BF575.A3 N33 2018 | DDC 155.9/37--dc23 LC record available at
https://lccn.loc.gov/2017028787
British Library Cataloguing-in-Publication Data
A CIP record is available from the British Library.

Printed in the United States of America
First Edition

http://dx.doi.org/10.1037/0000073-000

10 9 8 7 6 5 4 3 2 1

This book is dedicated to survivors of traumatic discrimination.
I hope this book will normalize their experiences
and help them in their healing processes.

Contents

Series Foreword

Exposure to traumatic events is all too common, increasing the risk for a range of significant mental problems, such as posttraumatic stress disorder and depression; physical health problems; negative health behaviors, such as smoking and excessive alcohol consumption; impaired social and occupational functioning; and overall lower quality of life. As mass traumas (e.g., September 11th; military engagements in Iraq and Afghanistan; natural disasters, such as Hurricane Katrina) have propelled trauma into a brighter public spotlight, the number of trauma survivors seeking services for mental health consequences will likely increase. Yet despite the far-ranging consequences of trauma and the high rates of exposure, relatively little emphasis is placed on trauma education in undergraduate and graduate training programs for mental health service providers in the United States. Calls for action have appeared in *Psychological Trauma: Theory, Research, Practice, and Policy* with such articles as "The Need for Inclusion of Psychological Trauma in the Professional Curriculum: A Call to Action," by Christine A. Courtois and Steven N. Gold (2009); and "The Art and Science of Trauma-Focused Training and Education," by Anne P. DePrince and Elana Newman (2011). The lack of education in the assessment and treatment of trauma-related distress and associated clinical issues at undergraduate and graduate levels increases the urgency to develop effective trauma resources for students and postgraduate professionals.

This book series, Concise Guides on Trauma Care, addresses that urgent need by providing truly translational books that bring the best of trauma psychology science to mental health professions working in diverse settings. To do so, the series focuses on what we know (and do not know) about specific trauma topics, with attention to how trauma psychology science translates to diverse populations (diversity broadly defined, in terms of development, ethnicity, socioeconomic status, sexual orientation, and so forth).

This series represents one of many efforts undertaken by Division 56 (Trauma Psychology) of the American Psychological Association to advance trauma training and education (http://www.apatraumadivision.org/68/ teaching-training.html). We are pleased to work with Division 56 and a volunteer editorial board to develop this series, which continues to move forward with the publication of this important guide on microaggressions by Kevin L. Nadal. As clinicians, researchers, and policymakers seek to better understand the impact of discrimination on mental health well-being, this monograph offers a practical and accessible guide for how to conceptualize microaggressions as traumatic experiences. Nadal's review on the empirical literature and clinical considerations regarding different types of microaggressions will be of great use to mental health professionals when working with individuals from minority backgrounds reporting trauma symptoms. Future books in the series will continue to address a range of assessment, treatment, and developmental issues in trauma-informed care.

Ann T. Chu
Anne P. DePrince
Series Editors

Preface

When I was a little kid, I used to hear my male relatives and friends say things like "That's so gay!" on a pretty regular basis. I would usually laugh along, hoping with all my might that they didn't know my secret. My parents and other adults in my life would tell me things like "Boys don't cry" or "Be a man!" which essentially was their way of telling me that being emotional was forbidden or a sign of weakness. Regarding my race and ethnicity, I can recall quite a few childhood memories in which I had similar feelings of pain and "otherness." Although my elementary school was fairly diverse, I sometimes felt like I was the only one with immigrant parents with accents or the only one who ate foods that others considered weird. I was called a few racial slurs when I was a kid, but I have blocked out the details. Perhaps my long-term memory is not working as well as it used to, or maybe in some ways, I forced myself to forget.

In high school, a few boys ridiculed me, almost daily—whispering "faggot" or screaming my name flamboyantly when I passed them in the halls. I taught myself to not show any reaction, and I decided to never tell anyone what was happening. Admitting that I was being bullied for being gay would mean I was admitting to being gay. I never felt so alone in my life.

Amidst this, I also started to encounter confusing incidents with racism. Some authority figures treated me in ways that made me feel like I was inferior, even though I knew I was smart. For example, a counselor once told me I shouldn't take certain honors classes because he didn't think I'd do well in them. Meanwhile, police officers stopped and questioned me many times, when I knew that I was not doing anything wrong. Some police officers asked me if I was in a gang, which especially annoyed me because I was a pretty nerdy kid who got good grades and did not get in trouble. While I certainly did not label these experiences as microaggressions, the fact that I can remember these instances so clearly, 20 or 30 years later, signifies that they were meaningful and caused some emotional reaction that I probably have not fully healed from.

This book has been one of the hardest pieces for me to write. Although I have written about multicultural issues in psychology (including microaggressions) for quite some time, writing this book was particularly daunting. At first, I thought it was writer's block; later, I concluded that I was stymied because writing about trauma can be traumatic. Recalling my personal history was not the source of stress for me; it was reading about historical events of trauma and writing case studies based on real people who have suffered from trauma. Further, knowing that many of my loved ones faced traumas in their lives—including child sexual abuse, sexual assault, hate violence, and other similar experiences—made writing about trauma feel even more grueling.

Despite this difficulty, I pushed through and wrote this book for a few reasons. First, I believe it is important for American society to discuss how oppression in its various forms affects all aspects of our lives, and how experiences with microaggressions and other types of discrimination can be very traumatic for many people. Second, I wanted to use my privilege as an educator and somewhat public figure to give voice to the many people in my life (and the people I have never met) whose experiences with discrimination have had overpoweringly negative impacts on their self-esteem, ability to thrive, or physical or mental health. Third, I hoped to teach clinicians and other helping professionals about the impact of microaggressions and trauma, so that they could better empathize with, and better serve, their clients. Finally, I wrote the book to do my small part to prevent future generations from experiencing microaggressions and discrimination. Unlike their predecessors, rising generations should not need to endure trauma, and they should not need to view the world as unfair or unsafe. If I can prevent that in any way, then pushing through my vicarious trauma and writing this book will have been worth it.

Acknowledgments

This book would not have been possible without the kind invitation of Ann Chu and Anne DePrince and the American Psychological Association Division 56: Division on Trauma Psychology. Thank you for recognizing that a book like this needed to be written. I am eternally grateful to my mentors, Derald Wing Sue, Jeannett Castellanos, Alfiee Breland, Elizabeth Fraga, Conrad Cathcart, Judy Patacsil, Fred and Dorothy Cordova, and so many others without whom I know I would not be where I am today. Thank you to my colleagues for sharing their clinical insight and wisdom needed for this book, especially Silvia Mazzula, Sidney Smith, David Rivera, Marcia Liu, Cara Jacobson, E. J. David, Helen Hsu, Jioni Lewis, Edith Arrington, Alicia del Prado, Richelle Concepcion, Andy Paves, Sophia Kong, Yael Nitkin-Kaner, Maureen Allwood, Preeti Chauhan, Deryn Strange, Marta Esquilin, and Risë Nelson. Thanks also to my research assistants (past and present), who have been diligent and passionate in our quest to understand how to decrease microaggressions in the world. *Maraming salamat* to my parents, Leo and Charity, for sacrificing so much to give me a better life, and thank you to my family and friends for grounding me. Thank you to my professional families: the Asian American Psychological Association (AAPA), the AAPA Divisions on Filipino Americans and LGBTQQ Issues, the Center for LGBTQ Studies, the LGBTQ Scholars of Color Network, and the Filipino American National Historical Society (FANHS). Finally, thanks to my husband, RJ Kaleo, and our four-legged son, Tiano, for loving me unconditionally and teaching me more than I ever thought was possible.

Microaggressions and Traumatic Stress

Introduction

By the end of the year in which I wrote this book, approximately 5,000 news articles had been written about *microaggressions*— or subtle forms of discrimination that are often unintentional and typically target people of historically marginalized groups. Major news outlets, such as *The New York Times, HuffPost,* and *Los Angeles Times,* as well as websites, such as Buzzfeed and Salon, discussed whether microaggressions were real or perceived, and whether discrimination was even still a problem in the United States. Microaggressions were described in a variety of contexts—ranging from the experiences of students of color at predominantly White campuses to controversial platforms voiced by presidential candidates. Some writers argued that microaggressions led to a "victimhood culture," whereas others debated about whether microaggressions were bad for business. Some people who perceived or encountered microaggressions aimed to vocalize and

http://dx.doi.org/10.1037/0000073-001
Microaggressions and Traumatic Stress: Theory, Research, and Clinical Treatment, by K. L. Nadal

validate the realities and impacts of such experiences; others wanted to vehemently deny the existence of microaggressions, their possible consequences, or both.

Although Pierce, Carew, Pierce-Gonzalez, and Willis (1978) first conceptualized microaggressions in the late 1970s, the concept did not become popularized until 2007, when a seminal article by D. W. Sue et al. was published in *The American Psychologist*. Over the next 5 years, one analysis found that 73 empirical studies had been published on the concept of racial microaggressions (Wong, Derthick, David, Saw, & Okazaki, 2014), and another analysis estimated that between 2010 and 2015, 35 peer-reviewed articles or dissertations focused on the concept of microaggressions that target lesbian, gay, bisexual, transgender, and queer (LGBTQ) people (Nadal, Whitman, Davis, Erazo, & Davidoff, 2016). Although most psychological concepts usually take decades for majority of academics and the mainstream to become familiar with, microaggressions quickly became a concept known throughout academia (most notably in psychology and higher education) and eventually became part of the mainstream vernacular. In fact, in 2017, the term *microaggressions* was officially added to the Merriam–Webster dictionary (Italie, 2017). Despite this growth in familiarity, naysayers have continued to invalidate others' perceptions of microaggressions, without acknowledging the abundance of empirical studies that support their existence and impact. Meanwhile, proponents have often used alternative or diluted versions of the term—resulting in further confusion and misunderstandings.

Throughout this book, I address the various controversies surrounding microaggressions that are debated through both the mainstream media and academia—exploring theoretical conceptualizations, research, and implications for clinical practice. I describe how microaggressions may have long-lasting effects on the psychological health of all people—especially individuals from historically oppressed groups and communities. Specifically, I discuss the ways in which microaggressions may lead to psychological trauma, notably for people who encounter discriminatory incidents regularly and intensely throughout their lives.

THE CHANGING FACE OF DISCRIMINATION IN THE UNITED STATES

Over the past 10 years, the United States has borne witness to a spectrum of historic incidents that changed the landscape of America. For instance, the election of President Barack Obama in 2008 and the U.S. Supreme Court's passing of same-sex marriage in 2015 both signified victories for historically marginalized communities. Decades prior, many people had never imagined a day that a Black American would be elected to the most powerful office in the country. Similarly, many lesbian, gay, bisexual, trans, and queer people never imagined that they would ever have the opportunity to legally marry the one they love and for their union to be recognized by the federal government. With the emergence of these monumental events, many people have hoped, or even believed, that discrimination would no longer be an issue in the United States and that all Americans would be treated as equals, regardless of their identities. Despite these optimistic viewpoints, many high-profile incidents demonstrate that discrimination is still alive, even rampant, in the United States. For instance, the Southern Poverty Law Center reported that in the month following the 2016 president election, violent hate crimes were at a record high—with an estimated 315 hate crimes targeting immigrants, 221 hate crimes toward Black people, 112 hate crimes toward Muslims, and 109 hate crimes toward LGBTQ people (Nadal, 2017).

Violence toward Black people has also remained steady across the United States. In 2013, the world watched as George Zimmerman was acquitted after killing Trayvon Martin, an unarmed 17-year-old Black American male in Florida. Shortly after, the #BlackLivesMatter movement was created and gained momentum—increasing awareness of anti-Black racism, as well as the disproportionately large number of Black people who have been murdered by police officers in the United States. Years following, the names Michael Brown, Eric Garner, Freddie Gray, Tamir Rice, Sandra Bland, Philando Castile, and Alton Sterling turned into social media hashtags and increasing awareness of the many Black people who died at the hands of police (Nadal, 2017).

Regarding sexism and violence toward women, the Centers for Disease Control and Prevention (CDC) estimates that about one in five American women (or 19.3%) will report being raped at some point in their lives and that close to half of American women (or 43.9%) will face some other form of sexual violence in their lifetime (Breiding et al., 2014). The U.S. Department of Justice reported that women in 2010 experienced rape or sexual assault at much higher rates than men: 2.1 incidents of rape or sexual assault per 1,000 women, compared with 0.1 per 1,000 men (Planty, Langton, Krebs, Berzofsky, & Smiley-McDonald, 2013). Further, the report stated that only 65% of rapes are reported to police (Truman & Langton, 2014). The CDC also estimated that at some point in their lives, one third of women will experience intimate partner violence and one sixth will experience stalking victimization (Basile et al., 2011). The United Nations Office on Drugs and Crime (2012) estimated that women and girls compose 75% of the 20 million total cases of human trafficking globally, with the majority involving sexual exploitation. As violence against women persists, many scholars have asserted that sexism has remained a normalized part of society (Nadal, Mazzula, & Rivera, 2017). For instance, when audiotapes were released of Donald Trump making lewd comments about women, many presumed his campaign would be ruined. Instead, he defeated his opponent Hillary Clinton—the first female presidential nominee of a major political party and who many pundits considered the most qualified presidential candidate in recent history (with her experience as secretary of state, senator, and First Lady).

In addition to racism and sexism, prevalence of violence toward LGBTQ people is also high. For instance, from 2012 to 2013, the years following the passing of legalized same-sex marriage in New York, anti-LGBTQ hate crimes increased. One prominent case involved the murder of Mark Carson, a 32-year-old gay Black man who was killed in New York City in May 2013. The assailant, Elliot Morales, accosted Carson and his boyfriend as they walked through the West Village of Manhattan, allegedly yelling homophobic slurs before shooting Carson point blank. A few months later, two men assaulted Islan Nettles (a Black, trans woman) in Harlem, after learning of her transgender identity; she died a few days later. These types of anti-LGBTQ hate violence cases occur all over the United States, with the Federal Bureau of Investigation (2014) revealing that about 21% of the total number of reported hate crimes in the United States target LGBTQ people. The National Coalition of Anti-Violence Programs (2013) reported a higher number—estimating that 32% of all hate crimes are directed toward LGBQ people and 10.5% toward transgender people. Given that the LGBQ and transgender populations compose only about 3.5% and 0.3% of the U.S. population (Gates, 2011), respectively, it is evident that LGBTQ people are targeted for hate violence at disproportionately higher rates.

Further, the research on anti-LGBTQ bullying also illustrates ways that heterosexist discrimination still persists. According to the 2013 National School Climate Survey (which surveyed 7,800 self-identified middle school and high school students), 85% of students reported being verbally harassed, and 65% of these students heard homophobic language "frequently" or "often" (Kosciw, Greytak, Palmer, & Boesen, 2014). Further, in comparison with LGBTQ students who reported being victimized at their school, LGBTQ students who were not harassed reported better grades, a greater motivation to attend college, and higher levels of self-esteem. It thus appears that being bullied greatly contributes to poorer outcomes for LGBTQ students and thus anti-LGBTQ bias is still a national issue.

Finally, despite the passage of the Americans With Disabilities Act of 1990 (ADA; 1991), people with disabilities (PWDs) encounter violence at much higher rates than those without disabilities. According to the U.S. Department of Justice, in 2013, the rate of nonfatal violent victimization (e.g., rape, sexual assault, robbery, aggravated assault, simple assault) was twice as high for PWDs (36 per 1,000) than for people without disabilities (14 per 1,000; Harrell, 2015). The same report indicated that PWDs accounted for 21% of all violent crimes (1.3 million incidents), despite only composing 14% of the U.S. population (Harrell, 2015). In 2013, about 24% of PWDs who were crime victims reported that they were targeted because of their disability, which was much higher than the 13% who reported similar sentiments in 2009 (Harrell, 2015). Regarding specific disabilities, people with cognitive disabilities, more than any other type of disability, were most likely to be targeted for violence. For every 1,000 people with a cognitive disability, 66.8 people report a violent incident, and 25.1 people report a serious violent incident (Harrell, 2015). Finally, about half of any violence toward PWDs (or 51%) occurs toward people with multiple disability types (Harrell, 2015), suggesting that having multiple disabilities increases risk of victimization.

SYSTEMIC DISCRIMINATION
IN AMERICAN SOCIETY

In addition to interpersonal violence and acts of overt discrimination, research supports that systemic discrimination persists in various sectors of contemporary American society. According to Zweigenhaft and Domhoff's (2014) analysis of the Fortune 500, only six CEOs were Black, 10 were Latino, and 10 were Asian American—accounting for only 5.2% of the total number of CEOs. The number of Fortune 500 female CEOs was also low; at the end of 2013, there were only 23 women CEOs (or 4.8% of the total number of CEOs)—almost all of whom were White. Given that the U.S. population consists of 13.6% Black Americans, 17.4% Latina/o/x Americans, and 5.4% Asian Americans (U.S. Census Bureau, 2015), and 50.8% are women (U.S. Census Bureau, 2010), the percentages of White and male CEOs are considerably disproportionate. Such numbers are especially bleak for women of color and other people with intersectional marginalized identities.

Socioeconomic status and wealth tends to be disproportionate for people of color and women. One study found that in 2010, White families were 6 times as wealthy as non-White families and White families earned, on average, about $2 for every $1 that Black and Latina/o/x families did (McKernan, Ratcliffe, Steuerle, & Zhang, 2013). In 2014, women's median weekly full-time earnings were 82.5% of men's weekly full-time earnings (Hegewisch, Ellis, & Hartmann, 2015), and Black and Latina women's weekly earnings were disproportionately lower than White men's (68.6% and 61.2%, respectively; U.S. Department of Labor, Bureau of Labor Statistics, 2015). So, although women are making relatively more money than they were a decade ago, disparities based on race and gender, especially for women of color, clearly still exist in the United States.

Systemic discrimination negatively affects LGBTQ people as well. Although same-sex marriage was legalized in the United States in 2015, no federal laws prevent LGBTQ people from being fired from their jobs on the basis of sexual orientation or gender identity (Feder & Brougher, 2013). As of 2016, 28 states lacked clear, fully inclusive protections for LGBTQ people; thus, in the majority of U.S. states, LGBTQ people can be fired from their jobs because of their sexual orientation or gender identity. Further, although President Obama signed the Matthew Shepard and James Byrd, Jr., Hate Crimes Prevention Act in 2009 (which made it a federal crime to assault individuals based on sexual orientation and/or gender identity), the majority of the 50 states do not recognize sexual orientation or gender identity as protected identity classes in hate crime legislation (Plumm, Terrance, & Austin, 2014).

Systemic discrimination may negatively affect PWDs as well, specifically regarding unemployment and poverty. In comparison with the 7.2% of the general population who are unemployed, approximately 14.7% of PWDs (who are interested in and eligible for work) are unemployed (U.S. Department of Labor, Bureau of Labor Statistics, 2014). Further, PWDs, on average, earn less than $25,000 per year, and about one fifth of people with severe disabilities live in poverty (Yee, 2011). Many PWDs report how health care facilities do not accommodate their needs (e.g., do not have proper equipment, do not have proper accessible entryways), and others believe health care providers are not sensitive in providing services and do not provide adequate services (Sharby, Martire, & Iversen, 2015). So, although the ADA was created to protect the civil rights of PWDs, access to health care and other resources is still not equitable or available.

MICROAGGRESSIONS IN EVERYDAY LIFE

Despite these examples of systemic and interpersonal discrimination, the United States has come a long way since the days of slavery and its aftermath. No longer is it legal for people to willfully initiate any type of violent attack, let alone any violence that is based on someone's race, gender, sexual orientation, ability status, religion, or any other identity group. For the most part, it is also generally socially unacceptable to be overtly biased and discriminatory, specifically if it involves inflicting any physical hurt or pain on other people. For example, in previous generations, it was common (or forgivable) for men to sexually assault women; however, current societal norms consider rape to be a horrendous and punishable act. Similarly, because most Americans do not participate in violent hate crimes, they view perpetrators of hate violence as bigots, racists, homophobes, or other similar labels.

Many authors have posited that American society has become more "politically correct" and that most people are aware of what is socially acceptable to say or do, particularly when it comes to issues related to race, gender, and religion (D. W. Sue, 2010b). Most White people tend to view themselves as "good" people, while classifying overtly discriminatory people (e.g., Ku Klux Klan members, neo–Nazis) and behaviors (e.g., hate crimes, racist jokes) as "bad" (D. W. Sue et al., 2007). Similarly, heterosexual and *cisgender* (i.e., people whose gender identity matches their assigned sex at birth) people who do not actively partake in homophobia or transphobia view themselves as fair and unbiased, without realizing the ways in which their heterosexist or transphobic biases may manifest in their language or behaviors (Nadal, 2013).

For the past several decades, psychology researchers have found that individuals' biases and prejudices manifest in more subtle and unconscious ways. In general, White people believe they do not have any racial biases and instead value racial and ethnic equality; yet, studies reveal that many White people still subconsciously hold negative feelings toward people of color or maintain implicit biases about these groups (Jost et al., 2009). For instance, although many White people may profess to not view Black people as inferior or criminal, they might struggle if their child were to date or marry a Black person. Similarly, although many heterosexual or cisgender people claim they do not hold any biases against LGBTQ people, they might have difficulty accepting it if their child came out as queer or transgender.

Because of implicit bias and the societal taboo of overt discrimination, scholars have described how "old-fashioned," or blatant, forms of discrimination are no longer commonplace, and that subtle discrimination emerges more frequently. Although there have been numerous terms to describe these phenomena (e.g., *modern racism, aversive racism, covert racism*), these subtle forms of discrimination more recently have been conceptualized as microaggressions (Nadal, 2011, 2013; D. W. Sue, 2010a; D. W. Sue et al., 2007). *Microaggressions* are verbal, behavioral, and environmental manifestations of bias; although they are often unintentional or unconscious, they communicate a spectrum of negative messages, primarily to people of historically marginalized groups. Research has found that microaggressions affect communities of color (see Wong et al., 2014, for a review), LGBTQ people (see Nadal et al., 2016, for a review), women (Capodilupo et al., 2010; Nadal, 2010), and PWDs (Keller & Galgay, 2010)—resulting in myriad psychological consequences, such as depression, anxiety, and trauma (Nadal, 2013; Nadal, Griffin, Wong, Hamit, & Rasmus, 2014; Torres & Taknint, 2015).

THE CONNECTION BETWEEN MICROAGGRESSIONS AND TRAUMA

Before understanding how microaggressions may be related to trauma, it is necessary to first clarify the definition of *trauma*. I provide two definitions—one offered by the *Diagnostic and Statistical Manual of Mental Disorders* (5th ed.; *DSM–5*), which is published by the American Psychiatric Association (2013), and the other by the *International Classification of Diseases* (10th ed.; ICD–10), which is published by the World Health Organization (WHO; 1992). Although the ICD–10 has been mandated for use in the United States by general health practitioners, the *DSM–5* tends to still be used more in the training of psychologists in the United States. Further, the 11th edition of the ICD (ICD–11) is expected to be released soon and to include more rigid definitions of trauma—potentially resulting in fewer post-traumatic stress disorder (PTSD) diagnoses (Sachser & Goldbeck, 2016). Thus, I offer both definitions and provide specific implications when applicable.

To fit the *DSM–5* criteria, a *traumatic event* involves "actual or threatened death, serious injury, or sexual violation" (American Psychiatric Association, 2013, p. 271). The trauma must be either directly felt by an individual (e.g., someone who is physically assaulted), witnessed by an individual (e.g., someone who watches a family member being killed), felt after learning that a traumatic event occurred to a loved one (e.g., someone who discovered their father died in the World Trade Center attacks), or endured after firsthand repeated or extreme exposure to aversive details of the traumatic event (e.g., a first responder who meets survivors and victims of brutal accidents or tragedies). When symptoms are pervasive and persist over time, the disturbance may cause significant distress or impairment in the person's life, including romantic or social relationships, work or school functioning, and basic everyday functioning (e.g., getting out of bed, bathing). The ICD–10 defined *trauma* as a "stressful event or situation of an exceptionally threatening or catastrophic nature, which is likely to cause pervasive distress in almost anyone" (WHO, 1992, p. 147). Although both the ICD–10 and *DSM–5* require a stressful situation as the main criteria, the *DSM–5* requires an emotional reaction to the stressful situation too. Previous research found that survivors of trauma often display many psychological symptoms, including, but not limited to, (a) shock, denial, or disbelief; (b) guilt, shame, or self-blame; (c) anger, irritability, mood swings; and (d) sadness and hopelessness (D. Sue, Sue, Sue, & Sue, 2015).

In many cases, incidents of overt discrimination and physical violence fit the criteria of trauma. When individuals are targeted by hate crimes, especially violent instances in which they are fearful for their lives, clinicians might easily classify the events as traumas because the encounters were frightening and caused significant distress. Similarly, when working with a survivor of a sexual assault, therapists are likely to assess for symptoms of PTSD. When people are diagnosed with PTSD, psychologists and other clinicians create various treatment plans to alleviate their symptoms; they also tend to validate or normalize survivors' reactions or PTSD symptoms as a natural and expected response to trauma.

On the other hand, when clients describe the persistent discrimination they face in their lives (which might not endanger their physical being in the same way that hate violence or sexual assault does), many therapists would not label these incidents as trauma. Although the discrimination is consistent, intense, and threaten individuals' feelings of safety, clinicians might argue that the event itself was not traumatic, hence negating the possibility of a PTSD diagnosis. Although the client might present with symptoms that are similar, or exactly equivalent, to PTSD symptoms, clinicians instead tend to impart a diagnosis of depression, anxiety, or some other unfitting psychological disorder. As a result, treatment may focus on changing the client's cognitive or behavioral reactions to discrimination, or exploring and analyzing the reasons the client is having such a negative reaction to discrimination. In other words, although people who experience PTSD are taught that external reasons are the causes for their mental illness, people who face discrimination are taught that internal reasons are why they are suffering.

When people face discrimination in their lives that is (a) intense, (b) extensive and enduring, (c) threatening to one's sense of safety, and (d) causal of symptoms that are aligned with PTSD (e.g., avoidance, dissociation), their experiences might be labeled as *traumatic discrimination*. Traumatic discrimination can manifest through blatant instances of victimization, which fit the current *DSM–5* criteria for trauma (e.g., racial hate crimes, sexual assault) but which may also occur through nonviolent overt discrimination (e.g., bullying, sexual harassment). Traumatic discrimination can also result from excessive and intense microaggressions (i.e., repeated exposure to subtle discrimination that persists throughout an individual's life), as well as from blatant and subtle forms of systemic microaggressions (e.g., enforced policies or practices in government or institution that continually marginalize certain groups of people). In this text, I also introduce the term *microaggressive trauma*, or the excessive and continuous exposure to subtle discrimination (both interpersonal and systemic) and the subsequent symptoms that develop or persist as a result. Although not all microaggressions are life threatening, they can certainly be pervasive and compromise one's sense of psychological and emotional safety, resulting in typical symptoms associated with trauma.

Further, I describe the ways that individuals' past histories with microaggressive trauma might manifest in their present lives and thus affect their daily life stressors and current mental health. Because many people do not fully heal from past traumas, they may internalize an array of negative emotions—including anger, sadness, worry, resentment, hopelessness, regret, and self-doubt. These emotions may then affect one's self-esteem, one's susceptibility to develop mental health problems, and even one's ability to succeed or function (Bedard-Gilligan et al., 2015). Additionally, people's present-day encounters with overt discrimination or microaggressions might serve as triggers to past memories of discrimination. When a person is triggered, they might experience a retraumatization, which causes psychological distress that is above and beyond whatever the current situation may entail (Duckworth & Follette, 2012). In other words, when people face microaggressions, they are not only reacting to the situations that are occurring in the moment but also might be reliving and reacting to unresolved, emotionally intense microaggressions of the past.

WHAT THIS BOOK COVERS AND WHOM IT IS FOR

Throughout this book, I argue that exposure to microaggressions may lead to symptoms, characteristics, or behaviors that are typically associated with PTSD: difficulty in concentrating; susceptibility to developing negative, internalized emotions (particularly of worthlessness, self-doubt, and distrust); and even potential difficulty in basic daily life functioning. Examples demonstrate how microaggressions can be intensely distressing if (and when) such discrimination is encountered on a frequent basis; if they are paired with past experiences of overt discrimination or violence; and if present-day microaggressions trigger past traumatic events with microaggressions or discrimination.

This book is grounded in two main theories. First, microaggression theory (D. W. Sue, 2010a, 2010b) is a philosophy that frames contemporary discrimination in the United States and many other parts of the world. I review the current theoretical and empirical literature involving microaggressions and discrimination toward various marginalized groups, as well as the impact of these types of discrimination on trauma and other mental health issues. Second, the book is also positioned in intersectionality theory (Crenshaw, 1989), which focuses on how the combination of one's race, sexual orientation, gender, gender identity, and other identities affect how one encounters, or copes with, microaggressions and trauma. In understanding intersectionalities, I also refer to critical race theory (Crenshaw, Gotanda, Peller, & Thomas, 1995), feminist theory (hooks, 2000), and queer theory (Jagose, 1996).

The book offers multiple examples of microaggressions and practical guidance on how to identify and deal with microaggressions as they occur. In Chapter 1, I cover what has traditionally been viewed as trauma, as well as ways that trauma may manifest differently, specifically in the context of overt systemic and interpersonal discrimination. Further, I introduce theoretical approaches to clinical treatment with trauma survivors of various marginalized identities. In Chapter 2, I discuss microaggression theory in detail—focusing on theoretical and empirical literatures that reveal the existence and impact of microaggressions. In Chapters 3 through 6, I discuss how microaggressive trauma may manifest uniquely in different communities and identity groups—namely focusing on people of color, LGBQ people, transgender people, and women. In these chapters, I provide examples from research, anecdotal experience, and media and popular culture to provide readers with examples of how microaggressive trauma may manifest, as well as to strategize different clinical approaches and interventions on how to address them. I also introduce several case studies (loosely based on real-life examples derived from my colleagues in the field). Cases include scenarios in which the encounters with discrimination are subtle, incidents in which the discrimination is much more overt, and instances in which there is a mix of overt and covert discrimination. Although a core identity may appear to be the focus of the discrimination or trauma, each case reflects intersectional identities too. Further, although not every identity group will be covered in this text, it is hoped that concepts can be applied to clients with other historically marginalized identities (e.g., PWDs, Muslims, people with mental illness). Finally, in Chapter 7, I conclude with recommendations on how to address microaggressive trauma—individually, institutionally, and systemically—while advocating for changes in psychology and education.

This book is intended for two types of audiences. First, practitioners and students in mental health fields (e.g., psychology, social work, counseling) will learn about how microaggressions can be traumatic and negatively affect mental health. Theory- and evidence-based recommendations or strategies are provided throughout, which I encourage practitioners to integrate into their therapeutic work with clients. Second, this book is written for people who have encountered microaggressions, as well as those who are committed to combatting them. Therapists may suggest this text to their clients who are struggling with microaggressive trauma and may need validation that their experiences are normalized. Educators, students, researchers, activists, and community leaders may benefit from the comprehensive reviews of discrimination and trauma, while gaining insight into the relationship between the two concepts. Regardless of the type of reader, it is my hope that the book will be a jumping point for more conversations in families, therapy rooms, classrooms, workplace environments, and anywhere that microaggressions may occur. By naming the relationship between microaggressions and trauma, we can begin to advocate for social change.

A Review of Trauma Literature
and Approaches

The American Psychiatric Association (2013) defined *trauma* as an emotional response to a catastrophic or frightening event. For a person to be clinically diagnosed with posttraumatic stress disorder (PTSD), the trauma experienced must include death, threatened death, actual or threatened serious injury, or actual or threatened sexual violence. Many types of hate victimization easily fit these criteria, resulting in a clear-cut clinical diagnosis of PTSD. As an example, imagine a transgender woman who is physically assaulted or severely beaten because of her gender identity (and who survives). Because she suffered an actual serious injury, and likely felt that her life was in serious danger, a clinician might easily label the incident as a trauma.

According to the *Diagnostic and Statistical Manual of Mental Disorders* (5th ed.; *DSM–5*; American Psychiatric Association, 2013), survivors of trauma also tend to develop psychological stressors and engage in avoidant

http://dx.doi.org/10.1037/0000073-002

Microaggressions and Traumatic Stress: Theory, Research, and Clinical Treatment, by K. L. Nadal
Copyright © 2018 by the American Psychological Association. All rights reserved.

behaviors, including having intrusive flashbacks to the event, experiencing terrifying nightmares, waking in the middle of the night in a panic or a sweat, and eluding places or objects that remind them of the attack. For instance, the aforementioned transgender woman might have difficulty concentrating at work because she is always remembering or visualizing the details of the attack. She might be extra sensitive and jumpy when encountering smells, sounds, or sights that remind her about the assault. She might also have difficulty in sleeping because she is constantly dreaming about being attacked or killed.

When clinicians recognize that their clients are survivors of trauma and that they might be suffering from typical symptoms of PTSD, they may use an array of trauma-focused techniques in their treatment plans, including eye-movement desensitization and reprocessing (EMDR), dialectical behavioral therapy (DBT), and trauma-focused cognitive behavior therapy. These types of treatments have empirical support for their ability to reduce the types of traumatic symptoms felt by an array of trauma survivors—including veterans, survivors of physical and sexual assault, individuals who have had nearly fatal experiences, and many others (Brown, 2008; Ford & Courtois, 2013; Lopez Levers, 2012). Although treatment for clients who are diagnosed with PTSD symptoms might be difficult and extensive, labeling such trauma and creating an appropriate treatment plan can assist survivors in healing and moving on with their lives. But what can be done when nonviolent or noncatastrophic events result in trauma symptoms? If the traumatic event does not match the *DSM–5* or *International Classification of Diseases* (10th ed.; ICD–10; World Health Organization, 1992) criteria, would a clinician know to utilize trauma-focused techniques? Do all psychologists and other psychotherapists believe that a traumatic event must be life threatening to treat it as such?

When people are verbally harassed or terrorized because of their religion, race, sexual orientation, gender, gender identity, ability, or some other identity, they might not necessary fear for their lives; however, they might fear for their safety. They may avoid certain places or neighborhoods that their tormentors reside in or frequent, to reduce the possibility of being harassed or physically hurt. They may even change their everyday functioning (e.g., dressing differently, taking a different route home from work or school) or give up interests or hobbies (e.g., quitting a sports team or afterschool club). They may also experience an array of psychological symptoms—including difficulty in concentrating, feeling edgy or consistently anxious, or even having nightmares and trouble sleeping. Thus, despite the presence of a life-threatening event, many people who are victimized might fit the criteria for trauma.

WHAT IS POSTTRAUMATIC STRESS DISORDER?

Before we examine the ways that discrimination can be traumatic and potentially result in symptoms related to PTSD, it is important to understand diagnostic criteria. When it was published in 2013, the *DSM–5* added a few criteria that differentiated trauma-related disorders from its earlier editions. For the first time, "Trauma- and Stressor-Related Disorders" were listed as separate from anxiety disorders (where they were previously categorized), given the wide range of traumatic stress and their major differentiations from traditional symptoms of anxiety. Additionally, the *DSM–5* added three new symptoms (for a total of 20 symptoms), included a new symptom cluster, and clarified that all symptoms must have begun or worsened after the trauma. Further, there are now two separate subtypes of PTSD: (a) PTSD preschool subtype (for children 6 years old or younger) and (b) PTSD dissociative subtype (which is accompanied by prominent dissociative symptoms).

The *DSM–5* definitions of *trauma* include exposure to (a) death, (b) threatened death, (c) actual or threatened serious injury, or (d) actual or threatened sexual violence. An individual can be diagnosed with PTSD if they had direct exposure to the trauma (e.g., a Muslim woman is the target of a violent hate crime), witnessed the trauma directly (e.g., a child witnesses her mother being sexually assaulted), experienced the trauma indirectly (e.g., a mother hears about her son's hate crime victimization), or had repeated or extreme indirect exposure to aversive details of a traumatic event (e.g., a first responder who tends to survivors of violent hate crimes or assaults). According to the *DSM*, the indirect exposure trauma cannot be experienced through films, books, photographs, or any other forms of media.

A *DSM* diagnosis also requires the presence of intrusion symptoms or the inability to keep memories or thoughts of a traumatic event from occurring. To fulfill this criterion, the client must report at least one of the following five symptoms: (a) recurrent, involuntary, and intrusive recollections of the traumatic event; (b) traumatic nightmares; (c) dissociative reactions or flashbacks, which may range from brief episodes to complete loss of consciousness; (d) intense or prolonged distress after exposure to traumatic reminders; or (e) noticeable physiological reactivity after exposure to trauma-related stimuli. Sometimes trauma survivors have nightmares that do not seem trauma-related, or they may not remember the content of flashbacks when they regain conscious awareness, thus not identifying the role of the trauma.

The second criterion for a PTSD diagnosis is the presence of avoidance symptoms, or the effortful attempt to evade any stimuli and triggers that may bring back memories of the trauma. To fulfill this symptom, the client must either persistently avoid (a) any trauma-related thoughts or feelings, or (b) any trauma-related external reminders (including, but not limited to, people, places, activities, objects, discussions, or situations that might be related to the trauma). For instance, an individual may do her or his best to avoid ever thinking about the traumatic events (typically unsuccessfully) or to circumvent people or places that might remind them of the event.

The third criterion for a *DSM* diagnosis is the presence of adverse changes in cognitions and mood that began or worsened after the traumatic event. The individual must indicate at least two of the following criteria: (a) incapacity to recollect key features of the traumatic event (not due to head injury or substance use), (b) persistent negative beliefs and expectations about oneself or the world (e.g., "I am worthless," "No one can be trusted"), (c) incessant self-blame or blame of others for being the cause of the traumatic event, (d) continuing negative trauma-related emotions (e.g., anger, fright, guilt, shame), (e) noticeably diminished interest in significant activities that occurred before the trauma, (f) feeling alienated from others, and (g) limited affect. Many symptoms under this cluster match similar symptoms of mood disorders, which is why it is important for clinicians to assess for the potential of traumatic events.

The fourth criterion for a PTSD diagnosis is the presence of changes in arousal and reactivity that are associated with the traumatic event. An individual must exhibit two out of six symptoms that must have started, or worsened, after the traumatic event: (a) irritable or aggressive behavior; (b) self-destructive or reckless behavior; (c) hypervigilance, or the enhanced state of sensory sensitivity to perceived threats; (d) exaggerated startle response; (e) problems in concentration; and (f) sleep disturbance. Although these symptoms must not be the result of substance use, medication, or any other physiological issue, substance use may enhance or interfere with some of these symptoms. For instance, if a survivor of trauma drinks alcohol, she or he may become intensely self-destructive or reckless.

To be diagnosed with PTSD, an individual must exhibit significant symptom-related distress or functional impairment. For more than 1 month, the person must also experience intrusion symptoms, avoidance, negative alterations in cognitions and mood, and alterations in arousal and reactivity. If a person encountered a traumatic event and the symptoms do not persist for more than 1 month, she or he might be diagnosed with acute stress disorder (ASD). To meet the criteria for ASD, an individual must (a) have undergone a traumatic event, as described by the aforementioned definitions of trauma used for PTSD; (b) exhibit nine of the above PTSD symptoms; and (c) exhibit symptoms that have lasted for at least 2 days but under 1 month. Further, the traumatic event must have caused some clinically significant distress or must have impaired the individual's social, occupational, or other important areas of functioning. Finally, it must be ruled out that all of the symptoms presented are not substance-induced or due to some other physiological problem.

A diagnosis of PTSD must also be differentiated from adjustment disorder, which typically occurs as a response to some sort of life stress (whether traumatic or not). The four types of adjustment disorder are depressed mood, anxious symptoms, disturbances in conduct, and mixed symptoms. Adjustment disorder has traditionally been used to classify an individual who does not quite meet the criteria for other diagnoses (e.g., depressive disorders, anxiety disorders, PTSD). Finally, when people are believed to have a stress-related disorder but do not quite fit the criteria for PTSD, ASD, or adjustment disorder, they may be diagnosed with "other specified trauma/stressor-related disorder" (American Psychiatric Association, 2013).

The ICD–10 has many similarities for diagnosis of PTSD as the *DSM–5* does but also has a few stark differences (Peters, Slade, & Andrews, 1999). First, regarding avoidance symptoms, only one symptom of actual or preferred avoidance is required (as opposed to two symptoms by the *DSM–5*). Further, for the ICD–10, a client must experience either (a) an inability to recall the event or (b) two or more of the following: sleep problems, irritability, concentration problems, hypervigilance, or exaggerated startled response. Finally, the ICD–10 requires that the symptoms occur within 6 months of the traumatic event, whereas a time onset is not required in the *DSM–5*. Given these, it appears that the ICD–10 generally has more flexible criteria for PTSD than does the *DSM–5*; however, the upcoming ICD–11 is expected to be more rigid than both the ICD–10 and the *DSM–5*—resulting in fewer PTSD diagnoses and, thus, fewer PTSD treatments (Sachser & Goldbeck, 2016).

A REVIEW OF INTERPERSONAL DISCRIMINATION AND TRAUMA

For more than two decades, several scholars have advocated for the expansion of clinical definitions of *trauma*, mainly in the *DSM* criteria for PTSD. Many psychologists have argued that trauma should not only refer to life-threatening or violent events but also include other catalysts of immense pain and suffering, such as oppression and discrimination. This section highlights previous literature that has examined four areas of research related to oppression and trauma: (a) insidious trauma, (b) race-based traumatic stress, (c) heterosexist traumatic stress, and (d) sexist and gender-based trauma.

Root first introduced her theory of insidious trauma in 1992, arguing that daily experiences of oppression (e.g., racial discrimination, poverty) are so widespread in historically marginalized communities that they can potentially inflict mild to severe psychological harm. According to this theory, insidious trauma is dangerous because it is chronic (i.e., it can occur at any given moment) and is long lasting (i.e., can persist over extended periods of time). Root also argued that because insidious trauma can be just as damaging and severe as traditionally conceptualized forms of the trauma (and because insidious trauma can lead to severe psychological distress), mental health practitioners should add insidious trauma (or any other trauma related to oppression) to the definition of and diagnostic criteria for trauma.

Following Root's (1992) work, several scholars wrote about insidious trauma and its effect on mental health. Loo et al. (2001) revealed the types of race-related stressors that Asian American Vietnam veterans encountered when they served in the military, especially during combat or in warzones. This finding represents the multiple types of trauma people face due to intersectional identities, particularly when identities seem to be in opposition of each other (e.g., Asian American veterans may be terrorized or harassed by their non-Asian fellow officers, while fearing being killed on enemy lines by Vietnamese soldiers). The personal narrative of a Filipino American veteran who served during the Vietnam War exemplifies this conflict:

> When I was at the base . . . it wasn't uncommon for my "own" soldiers to turn on me. I was called a "gook" pretty often by the White and Black American soldiers. It wasn't every day, but sometimes it was several times a day. Once in a while, someone would say something like "Hey boy, where did you get that uniform?" I just tried to ignore it. I guess that I understood that they were taking their frustrations out on me—someone who looks like the "enemy." So, to avoid this altogether, I hung out with the Australian soldiers who were able to recognize that I was Filipino, that I was American, and that I wasn't the enemy. (Tabaco, 2010, p. 247)

Facing the atrocities of war is daunting in itself. However, to navigate racism in addition to combat-related traumas can be remarkably distressing and laborious.

In the mid-2000s, several scholars shifted the conversation and began to theorize and study the concepts of race-based trauma and race-based traumatic stress. Bryant-Davis (2007) defined race-based trauma as involving one of the following traits: (a) an emotional injury that is racially motivated and targets a person or group; (b) a race-related stressor that interferes with a person's ability to cope; (c) a racially motivated, interpersonal stressor that causes physical injury or a threat to integrity; or (d) a racially motivated interpersonal or systemic stressor that causes psychological distress. Carter (2007) described how race-based traumatic stress should not be classified along with other *DSM* examples of trauma but instead should form its own category, given its distinct focus on emotional reactions of trauma rather than life-threatening aspects. Carter et al. (2013) created the Race-Based Traumatic Stress Scale (RBTSS) to provide a baseline for understanding a client's experiences with and reactions to the trauma. Using the RBTSS, Carter and Sant-Barket (2015) indicated that people who experienced racial events as traumatic versus stressful are more likely to undergo a behavioral or personality-related change as a result of the event. Further, trauma symptoms and reactions within 1 month after the event correlate with individuals' recent trauma symptoms—indicating how trauma symptoms are pervasive and can last over time.

Although the literature regarding the effects of heterosexist or transphobic trauma on lesbian, gay, bisexual, transgender, and queer (LGBTQ) people is scant, studies have supported that LGBTQ people report more frequent exposure to traumatic life experiences (and subsequently a higher prevalence of PTSD or other traumatic stress symptoms) than their heterosexual or cisgender counterparts (Balsam, Rothblum, & Beauchaine, 2005; Roberts, Austin, Corliss, Vandermorris, & Koenen, 2010). Shipherd, Maguen, Skidmore, and Abramovitz (2011) shared that in a study with 97 transgender women, almost all (98%) reported experiencing at least one traumatic event in their lifetimes and most participants (91%) indicated multiple traumatic events in their lives. Almost half of their sample (42%) reported that at least one of the events was induced by transphobic bias, and almost one fifth (17.8%)

met the *DSM* criteria for PTSD. Second, in a study with 528 lesbian, gay, and bisexual youth, (a) nearly 80% of the sample reported instances of verbal abuse, (b) 11% and 9% revealed histories of physical and sexual abuse, (c) 9% fulfilled *DSM* criteria for a PTSD diagnosis, and (d) PTSD symptoms were directly related to sexual orientation victimization and gender nonconformity (D'Augelli, Grossman, & Starks, 2006). Some studies have revealed that LGBTQ people experience trauma that fits *DSM* criteria while exhibiting traumatic symptoms more aligned with insidious trauma (e.g., Bandermann & Szymanski, 2014; Szymanski & Balsam, 2011).

Finally, previous research indicates that women, in general, are 2 to 3 times more likely than men to be diagnosed with (or meet criteria for) PTSD (Kimerling, Weitlauf, Iverson, Karpenko, & Jain, 2013; Tolin & Foa, 2006). Despite this higher prevalence, women actually experience fewer traumatic events than men overall (Norris, Foster, & Weishaar, 2002). Further, when women and men undergo the same type of traumatic event (e.g., both survive a natural disaster), women still develop PTSD symptoms at much higher rates than men (Tolin & Foa, 2006). One explanation for the gender discrepancies in PTSD is gender socialization, which results in different coping styles for men and women. For instance, men who are exposed to trauma might turn to substance use or aggressive behavior, whereas women might be more likely to express their emotions and exhibit depression and anxiety (Tolin & Breslau, 2007). Another explanation for gender disparities in PTSD is that women report chronic hypervigilance, due to their valid concerns for safety or fears of being sexually objectified or assaulted by men (Fairchild & Rudman, 2008; Watson, Marszalek, Dispenza, & Davids, 2015). Because of this preexisting fear, also referred to as *physical safety anxiety* (Fredrickson & Roberts, 1997), women's PTSD symptoms may be exacerbated when they actually do face a trauma or psychological distress. Finally, one study indicated that women who experience sexual harassment in the workplace might exhibit traumatic stress symptoms (Palmieri & Fitzgerald, 2005), and another study revealed a correlation between everyday sexism and PTSD symptoms, specifically for women who reported more frequent experiences with sexist degradation (Berg, 2006).

A REVIEW OF SYSTEMIC
AND COLLECTIVE TRAUMA

Now that we understand the various ways that interpersonal encounters with trauma can affect mental health, this section reviews the ways in which trauma can affect groups, communities, and even entire societies. First, *historical trauma* is defined as "a complex and collective psychological distress that is experienced over time and across generations of a group of people who share an identity, affiliation, or circumstance" (Mohatt, Thompson, Thai, & Tebes, 2014, p. 128). Literature on historical trauma has focused on experiences of Native Americans (Brave Heart & DeBruyn, 1998), Holocaust survivors (Kellermann, 2001), Native Hawaiians (Pokhrel & Herzog, 2014), and other groups who share a history of violence, victimization, colonization, or genocide. Due to slavery and systemic racism, Black Americans may feel a historical trauma that still has implications in present times. For instance, when Trayvon Martin was killed in 2012 (and George Zimmerman was found "not guilty" in 2013), many Black Americans reported a collective sense of psychological distress and emotional pain. Although they may not have known Trayvon Martin or his family personally, they empathized deeply, as though they did—perhaps because of their own fears that their innocent loved ones might be killed too or knowledge that another unarmed Black teenager was brutally murdered and whose assailant went free.

Historical trauma has also been found in LGBTQ communities. Herek and Berrill (1992) wrote that anytime a hate crime is committed, the event communicates "a warning to all gay and lesbian people to stay in 'their place,' the invisibility and self-hatred of the closet" (p. 3). To obtain empirical support for these concepts, Herek, Gillis, and Cogan (1999) surveyed LGBQ participants and found that individuals (who may or may not have ever been targeted for hate violence) reported multiple psychological stressors (e.g., being fearful of crimes, feeling vulnerable, viewing the world as a less benevolent place) at significantly higher rates than their heterosexual counterparts. Noelle (2002) referred to this phenomenon as a "ripple effect" that occurs when LGBTQ people learn about violence or hate crimes against people with shared similar sexual orientations and gender identities. Even when LGBTQ people are not directly involved in traumatic events, they lose fundamental assumptions of benevolence and meaningfulness of the world, which negatively affects their mental health. For instance, in 2016, when 49 people (mostly Latinx) were killed at Pulse—an LGBTQ nightclub in Orlando, Florida—many LGBTQ people (especially LGBTQ people of color) experienced significant distress and grief. Some developed PTSD symptoms, and others began to be hyper-vigilant and cautious of the world.

Related to historical trauma is *collective trauma*, which is defined as a group's shared sense of psychological distress because of witnessing or observing a terrifying event or tragedy (Frantz, 2014). Collective trauma can affect specific communities or groups but is often used to describe psychological distress experienced by entire societies or countries. Some examples of collective trauma include the shared sense of loss, grief, or distress that most Americans felt after the September 11th World Trade Center attacks in 2001 or the Boston Marathon bombings in 2013. A systematic review on 27 collective trauma studies ($N = 8,011$) indicated that when people experience collective trauma, they develop PTSD symptoms and poorer health, most notably when they have low self-efficacy (Luszczynska, Benight, & Cieslak, 2009). A study examining collective trauma after 9/11 found that greater exposure to graphic media images predicted increased PTSD symptoms and poorer physical health (Silver et al., 2013). Yet, it must be noted that the *DSM* declares that trauma cannot be experienced solely from any type of media.

Although historical and collective trauma are similar in nature, historical trauma is described as being felt most by people of historically marginalized groups, whereas collective trauma is typically characterized as being felt by a more general population. As an example, in 2015, Dylann Roof, a White male, killed nine innocent people at the Mother Emanuel Methodist Church in Charleston, South Carolina. Although some media covered the event and its aftermath, news reporters did not label the incident as a terrorist attack, even though it fit all of the criteria (i.e., Roof admitted to wanting to start a race war and did not personally know the victims). Further, although more people were killed in the incident than in the Boston Marathon, the mass shooting is simply not treated with the same regard or reverence, in that it was not viewed as a "national tragedy" but rather as a tragedy for the Black community. In this way, national tragedies seem to be defined as events in which White people are killed.

Vicarious trauma involves the ways that an individual can indirectly encounter trauma and develop symptoms usually felt by a direct survivor of trauma (McCann & Pearlman, 1990). Examples include people who learn of loved ones undergoing a traumatic event (e.g., parents who learn their child was murdered, tortured, or sexually abused) or people who are repeatedly exposed to trauma (e.g., first responders, mental health practitioners). Although their symptoms may not be as intense as those felt by direct trauma survivors, their symptoms can be painful and disruptive. If the individual identifies as part of the targeted group (e.g., a transgender clinician who works with transgender survivors of hate violence), the trauma may be even more intense, as the person fits criteria for both vicarious trauma and historical trauma.

Another related concept is *transgenerational trauma*, or the idea that trauma manifests across various generations in a family, above and beyond the generation of the original survivor of the trauma (Lev-Wiesel, 2007). For instance, although many children who lost parents on 9/11 were not born before the day of the tragedy and do not have direct memories from that day, they may still exhibit traumatic symptoms as a result of observing the pain and suffering felt by family members who were present. Specific to oppression, when people belong to groups that have been victimized (e.g., Black Americans, Native Americans, Japanese Americans in internment camps, Native Hawaiians) and also have a history of trauma in their families (e.g., a grandparent was killed because of hate violence, a parent was victimized by sexual abuse), they can report distress from both transgenerational and historical trauma.

ADVOCACY FOR A NEW DEFINITION OF TRAUMA

Over the past decade, many practitioners have advocated for new definitions of trauma. For instance, Helms, Nicolas, and Green (2010) argued that individuals (especially White people) fail to view racism and ethnoviolence as life-threatening traumas because of a lack of awareness of historical context and the invisibility of violence in present-day forms of discrimination. In other words, because present-day White people are less likely to be violent toward people of color and because they do not remember (or choose not to remember) the racist history of the United States, many White people may believe that racism no longer exists. When people of color discuss encounters with racism, some White people label them as being paranoid or hypersensitive, instead of acknowledging how their reactions to racism can be natural or expected responses to trauma. Similarly, Bryant-Davis and Ocampo (2005) cited reasons that psychologists and other practitioners might be hesitant, unreceptive, or oppositional to labeling racism (or other forms of discrimination) as a form of trauma. First, some clinicians accept *DSM–5* or ICD–10 criteria as the field's standard and do not feel the need challenge it. Second, some people believe labeling racism as a form of trauma would diminish or delegitimize the severity of other traumas (e.g., if racism is labeled a trauma, it would diminish traumatic stress associated with combat veterans or survivors of violent sexual assault). Third, people from historically marginalized groups who speak up against oppression are viewed as "angry" or "sensitive"—as opposed to survivors of diagnostic trauma, whose reactions are "normal" responses to events that were "out of their control." Such sentiments are still common in that (a) many White psychologists do not feel compelled to challenge the status quo; (b) many still deny the existence or severity of racism; and (c) instead of validating their reactions, many blame people of color for reacting to racism.

Despite these arguments, when the new *DSM–5* was released in 2013, it did not include discrimination as an official part of its definition of trauma. However, one major change was that PTSD or ASD no longer included symptoms of fear, helplessness, or horror, which were prior requirements in previous *DSM* revisions. Thus, the *DSM* now leaves more room for interpretation, allowing for clinicians to decide whether encounters with discrimination are traumatic events that might possibly lead to symptoms of PTSD or ASD. Although this is a positive step, some advocates argue that not labeling racism, sexism, or heterosexism explicitly in the *DSM–5* enables practitioners with less cultural competence (i.e., therapists who might not be committed to social justice or who only have surface-level understandings of systemic discrimination) to continue to exclude discrimination as a form of trauma.

Culturally Competent Treatment Approaches to Trauma

In recent years, psychologists have offered culturally competent approaches in working with trauma survivors, particularly those from historically marginalized communities. Examples include race-based trauma therapy (Bryant-Davis & Ocampo, 2006), racial trauma recovery (Comas-Díaz, 2016), feminist therapy (Brown, 2008), and queer-affirmative phase-oriented psychotherapy (Rosenberg, 2000). Although these theories may have been written initially for specific groups, components of each theory have implications for other marginalized groups.

Race-Based Trauma

Bryant-Davis and Ocampo (2006) recommended several approaches when working with survivors of race-based trauma, with an emphasis on understanding a client's trauma history and how the therapeutic relationship and therapeutic process can influence outcomes. In this model, practice can integrate the following steps (regardless of theoretical orientation). First, therapists must acknowledge the racist incident as a trauma—which validates to clients that they were not randomly targeted but that the incident was part of a greater systemic problem. Second, they encourage clients to share their trauma within environments where they are not judged or questioned. Third, therapists can assess clients' current level of safety (e.g., how threatening it would be for them to return to a traumatic environment) and self-care (e.g., how able clients are able to cope or avoid self-harm). Fourth, therapists allow clients to grieve or mourn any losses associated with the trauma (e.g., feelings of humiliation, shame, shock; physical injuries that occurred). Fifth, therapists guide clients in exploring shame, self-blame, and internalized oppression. Finally, therapists assist clients in connecting to and managing their anger; they also guide clients in developing both coping skills (e.g., strategies to employ when feeling triggered) and resistance skills (e.g., empowering oneself, advocating for justice). Bryant-Davis and Ocampo also suggested that therapists consider methods such as art therapy, movement therapy, and storytelling. For clients who may have a strong sense of spirituality or religion, treatment can also include guiding clients in exploring healthy coping mechanisms through spiritual practices.

Racial Trauma Recovery

Comas-Díaz (2016) built on the work of race-based trauma and added a few more elements when working with survivors of racial trauma. Her racial trauma recovery model includes five steps: (a) assessment and stabilization, (b) desensitization, (c) reprocessing, (d) psychological decolonization, and (e) social action. In the assessment phase, by providing a safe environment and validation, clinicians encourage clients to provide testimony of their experiences with racial trauma. She also recommended evaluating the severity of a client's trauma with a measure such as Carter et al.'s (2013) RBTSS. Through desensitization, therapists can assist clients as they relive their traumas in therapy, by using traditional trauma techniques, such as EMDR or safe-place imagery. However, Comas-Diáz also encouraged integrating ethnic and indigenous healing or approaches that are aligned with a client's ethnic or cultural background. In the reprocessing phase, the therapist assists clients in searching for meaning and posttraumatic growth. For instance, therapists guide clients in reframing traumatic incidents as "wisdom-enhancing" sources of empowerment. Through decolonization, therapists address clients' colonial mentalities—or the ways that clients have internalized their own cultural groups to be inferior and dominant groups as superior. One goal could be for the client to develop a critical consciousness by unpacking how systemic oppression affects their self-esteem and their functioning. Finally, in the social action stage, the clients learn to advocate for social change (e.g., getting involved in their community organizations, voicing their experiences survivors of trauma, mentoring other survivors).

Feminist Approaches to Therapy

Although feminist therapy has evolved since its conception in the 1970s, its main tenets include therapist awareness of systemic sexism and its impact on gender roles and relationships, and advocacy for social action, egalitarianism, and the empowerment of women and other historically disenfranchised groups (Brown, 2008). Specific to trauma, feminist therapists understand that survivors develop behavioral symptoms as a result of the trauma, and that systemic oppression may negate their healing and recovery (Brown, 2008). Further, although people may presume that feminist therapies are only effective for cisgender women, the treatment can be applied to a multitude of groups, including men (Mejía, 2005), transgender and gender nonconforming people (Richmond, Burnes, Singh, & Ferrara, 2017), and others.

Feminist theorists have provided several recommendations for working with survivors of trauma. First, therapists guide clients in learning how to advocate for themselves, specifically in working with people and systems that historically have been biased or discriminatory. One way to do this is to assist clients in developing a feminist critical consciousness, or an understanding of the ways that systemic sexism (and other forms of oppression) has shaped various aspects of the client's life. In understanding oppression, clients may understand that their trauma is based on a bigger societal problem, which may empower them to advocate for change. Feminist therapists may also help clients to develop a survivor's identity (Richmond et al., 2017), which may help them unpack emotions related to their trauma, while also encouraging clients to become role models to other survivors who still self-blame. Therapists may facilitate clients in self-reflection activities, such as journal-writing or art therapy; therapists may also use traditional methods of cognitive behavioral therapy, such as disputing irrational beliefs and encouraging positive self-talk (Brown, 2008).

Queer-Affirmative Phase-Oriented Psychotherapy

Although little research has examined trauma approaches for LGBTQ people, some authors have described integrating mainstream treatment approaches with LGBTQ-affirmative theories. For instance, Rosenberg (2000) discussed how one can use phase-oriented therapy with gay male survivors of trauma. The three main phases that are typically a part of this treatment include (a) stabilization and symptom reduction, (b) treatment of traumatic thoughts or memories, and (c) integration of new self and relational development. With each stage, the queer-affirming therapist may consider several factors that may influence treatment. For instance, in examining meanings and cognitive distortions, therapists can guide clients in understanding how internalized homophobia or gender role norms have influenced their behaviors and their feelings about themselves. Further, queer-affirmative therapists must be flexible and knowledgeable in how behavior may manifest differently in each stage. For instance, non-monogamous sexual behaviors are often shamed in general society but are more accepted in gay male communities; accordingly, therapists must not assume such behavior to be deviant without first asking clients the meanings of their behaviors, or considering the norms of queer communities.

CASE STUDY

Sara was a 34-year-old heterosexual White, Jewish American woman who sought therapy to discuss anxieties related to her romantic relationship. Her parents, Eileen and Ryan, have been married for 40 years, and she has an older sister named Debra. She grew up in a traditional Jewish household, within a larger predominantly Jewish community in the Mid-Atlantic region of the United States. When Sara's paternal grandfather died when she was 7 years old, her grandmother, Helen, moved in with her family. Having lived together in the same house for 10 years before Sara moved for college, Sara and her grandmother developed a close relationship.

In her first therapy session, Sara shared that her "Bubbie Helen" was a Holocaust survivor who was born in Germany in the 1930s. When Helen was 9 years old, her family was forced out of their home, and she and her mother were separated from her father and her two older brothers. She described that they were forced to board separate buses, that they were not allowed to say goodbye, and that she never saw them again. She later learned that her brothers were sent to one of the Auschwitz concentration camps and that both brothers were killed after attempting to organize a revolt. Helen was able to stay with her mother and her aunt for a short time, but she witnessed her mother being shot by a Nazi soldier when he accused her of being defiant. Her aunt became her guardian, and they escaped to Switzerland. They eventually moved to England, where Helen spent the majority of her adolescence. She immigrated to the United States in her late teens, where she later met her husband (who was also Jewish but not

33

a Holocaust survivor) and raised her children (who later married Jewish spouses too).

When Sara was 16 years old, she and her family went to the Holocaust Museum in Washington, DC, where she describes "crying the entire time." In college, she wanted to learn more about the Holocaust, so she enrolled in multiple classes and minored in Holocaust studies. She read every book and watched every film that she could find about the Holocaust—admitting that each made her cry but helped her feel more closely connected to her grandmother's experience. Every summer, she volunteered at a camp for Jewish youth; she loved teaching them about Judaism and encouraging them to develop proud Jewish identities. When Sara had just finished college, her grandmother was diagnosed with terminal cancer, which prompted Sara to move back home. Before she passed, her grandmother made Sara promise to never forget the Holocaust and to always honor her Jewish identity. Her grandmother hinted that it would make her so happy if Sara married "a nice Jewish boy" and raised her children in the Jewish faith.

Six years ago, Sara met Jason, a young multiracial, Catholic man of Italian American and Puerto Rican heritage. Although Sara was not interested in dating someone who was not Jewish, she thought he was very attractive, funny, and smart, so she agreed to go on a date with him. They dated for several months and fell in love. They moved in together after a year of dating, but because of his non-Jewish identity, Sara never thought their relationship would last. Sara mentioned in therapy that she also believed that Jason does not quite understand how important her religion and family history are to her, and that she often found herself trying to educate him about the Holocaust. Although Jason had never said anything anti-Semitic or invalidating, he also never expressed any real interest in learning more about Judaism or in feeling an emotional connection to the Holocaust. Sara tried to learn more about Jason's Catholic traditions and family history (as a way of demonstrating her love for him), but he assured her his religious identity lacks personal salience.

Sara sought therapy because she felt lost and did not know what to do. She loved Jason (who has been recently hinting at marriage), but she also remembered her promise to her grandmother. Further, because Sara was in her mid-30s, she worried that if she broke up with Jason, she would not find anyone else and lessen her chance to have a baby. She also felt guilty because everyone in her family had Jewish spouses. So, if she did indeed marry Jason, she felt she would be letting everyone down.

CASE STUDY DISCUSSION AND CLINICAL RECOMMENDATIONS

Many issues must be considered in Sara's case, specifically involving historical trauma and transgenerational trauma. Sara was affected by historical trauma in that she is a Jewish American woman who has learned about the atrocities that Jewish people encountered during the Holocaust, including captivity, brutality, murder, and annihilation. However, Sara was also distressed by transgenerational trauma, in that her grandmother faced trauma firsthand and many relatives (e.g., her great grandparents and grand-uncles) were killed during this time. Both types of trauma can be daunting, but being able to relate to both might be exceptionally painful.

Sara's case also brings up the notion of transgenerational transmissions of trauma, in which psychological stressors, such as guilt or shame, can persist for several generations (de Mendelssohn, 2008). Although Sara is legitimately passionate about her Jewish faith, she also feels guilty about the promise that she made to her grandmother about marrying a Jewish man. She genuinely loves her boyfriend, but she feels guilty that she would not be marrying someone who comes from her same Jewish background. And because she does not have any role models of other family members who have married non-Jewish people, she may fear being ostracized or stigmatized if she married Jason and had children who were not raised Jewish.

Further, Sara's case demonstrates how trauma might not necessarily fit diagnostic criteria for PTSD. As far as the reader can tell, Sara has not encountered any life-threatening event in which she was personally exposed to danger or catastrophic circumstances. She has learned about the trauma her grandmother endured; however, such trauma occurred almost 75 years ago, and psychologists and other clinicians might not view learning about it as being as harrowing or intense as learning that a loved one suffered from a traumatic event in the recent past. Similarly, although Sara claims that she has a strong emotional reaction to anything she sees or reads that is related to the Holocaust, the *DSM* clearly states that trauma must not be experienced through films, books, photographs, or any other forms of media. Accordingly, Sara's presenting issues might not be viewed through the lens of trauma, which may result in a clinician's overlooking the salience of trauma in Sara's life.

This case also illustrates the importance of understanding intersectional identities and extraneous factors, in that there are multiple other identities and experiences that influence the ways Sara was affected by trauma. For example, because Sara was a woman in her 30s, she worries that her age may influence whether she can be a mother. Perhaps if a Jewish man were put in the same situation, or if Sara were younger, the pressure would not seem as intense. Further, if Sara grew up in a home or community where religion was not heavily emphasized, it is possible that the historical or transgenerational trauma would not feel as intense for her.

One clinical approach that could be implemented in working with Sara is feminist therapy (Brown, 2008)—which would encourage Sara to develop a critical feminist consciousness while understanding how systems have influenced her behaviors. A feminist therapist might ask Sara to explore how anti-Semitism may have influenced her grandmother's expectations—particularly regarding her life choices and gender roles. A feminist therapist might encourage her to write journals to sort through her emotions or potentially might invite Sara to write a letter to her grandmother to connect to direct emotions that she might have. Additionally, a feminist therapist might encourage Sara to further develop her social justice and community involvement in her religious community, which seemed to be a source of healing for her.

Finally, using feminist therapy, the identities of Sara's therapist can also affect Sara's treatment. Although Sara did not indicate any preference for a type of therapist, potential clinicians must consider how their own identities might influence Sara's ability to share and be completely honest in the therapeutic context. Relatedly, psychodynamic or relational psychotherapists might recognize how their different identity groups might affect both transference and countertransference. *Transference* is defined as a client's unconscious thoughts or feelings about people or experiences outside of a therapy session that are redirected toward a counselor or clinician. Conversely, *countertransference* is a counselor's or clinician's unconscious thoughts or feelings about people or experiences outside of a therapy session that are unconsciously redirected toward a client (D. Sue, Sue, Sue, & Sue, 2015). Analyzing transference and counter-transference can be helpful in building a rapport with Sara and can help a therapist and client recognize potential unresolved issues, gender roles, or power dynamics that may manifest in Sara's life. For instance, if her therapist were an older Jewish woman, Sara may be reminded of her grandmother, which might deter her from fully exploring her guilt and other negative feelings; conversely, if Sara's therapist were a young, non-Jewish man, she might be hesitant to disclose her feelings, in fear that the therapist would side with Jason, judge her, or both.

2

What Are Microaggressions?

The term *microaggressions* was first introduced in the 1970s. Micro-aggressions were defined as "subtle, stunning, often automatic, and nonverbal exchanges which are 'put downs'" (Pierce, Carew, Pierce-Gonzalez, & Willis, 1978, p. 66). The term was used to describe subtle discrimination that Black Americans faced, primarily regarding stereotypical media portrayals. For the next 30 years or so, few articles mentioned microaggressions at all. In 2000, one study highlighted the spectrum of microaggressions that students of color encountered on college campuses (Solórzano, Ceja, & Yosso, 2000), and another article discussed the types of microaggressions Latina/os experience in the criminal justice system (DeJesus-Torres, 2000). Other than these, limited literature used or cited the term until D. W. Sue et al. (2007) reintroduced the concept of racial microaggressions in *American Psychologist*.

http://dx.doi.org/10.1037/0000073-003
Microaggressions and Traumatic Stress: Theory, Research, and Clinical Treatment, by K. L. Nadal
Copyright © 2018 by the American Psychological Association. All rights reserved.

Perhaps the concept of microaggressions did not take root imme-diately because of the overt racism that was still flourishing throughout society. In the 1980s, it was somewhat acceptable for White people to be blatantly racist through language, jokes, or even hiring practices. In fact, the term *hate crime* did not enter the American vernacular until the 1980s, when some states passed legislation to prosecute crimes in this manner. Even then, hate crimes were underreported and unknown—as evidenced by the lack of media attention to the 1982 murder of Vincent Chin—an Asian American killed by his coworker in Detroit for race-related reasons (Kurashige, 2002).

In the 1990s, many racialized incidents were reported in the media, which led to many dialogues about race relations in many sectors of American society. First, when videotape emerged of Los Angeles Police Department (LAPD) officers beating Rodney King in 1991, many White Americans first became aware of police brutality—an issue that many Black people knew had existed since the times of slavery. When the LA Riots of 1992 arose (directly after the aforementioned LAPD officers were acquitted on all charges of excessive force), the media portrayed Black Americans as thieves and criminals, perpetuating stereotypes of Black people. Conversations about race continued in the 1990s with the trial of O. J. Simpson, the emergence of gang violence primarily in working class Black communities, an increase in the numbers of immigrants from Asia and Latin America, and the various efforts to eliminate affirmative action. In 2001, the national dialogue moved in a different direction after the 9/11 World Trade Center attacks, when people began to overtly stereo-type Muslims (and others presumed to be Muslim) as terrorists. Thus, conversations on microaggressions may have seemed pointless because racism, xenophobia, and Islamophobia were so blatant.

The state of sexism followed a very similar trajectory. Although the term *sexual harassment* was coined in 1975, most Americans did not know the term until 1991, when Anita Hill testified about her experiences of Clarence Thomas during his U.S. Supreme Court nomination hearing. Up until then, many women commonly endured sexual harassment in the workplace—experiences that were not typically reported, let alone punished. Women were also victimized by sexual assault at much higher rates than today, and the prevalence of unreported sexual assaults was much higher. If women had a difficult time in reporting these incidents of blatant sexual harassment or sexual violence, perhaps it seemed trivial to address their encounters with microaggressions.

Similarly, during the 1970s and 1980s, many lesbian, gay, bisexual, transgender, and queer (LGBTQ) people did not express their sexual orientation or gender identity because of the fear of violence, rejection, or isolation. Despite the Stonewall Uprising of 1969, which is said to be the start of the LGBTQ civil rights movement, homophobia and transphobia were rampant throughout the United States. LGBTQ people who were "out" during this time often lost their jobs, were banished from their families, and/ or were stereotyped as sexual predators. Accordingly, many LGBTQ people were cautious and lived double lives (e.g., a gay man "passed" as straight in the daytime but frequented gay bars at night), while others never allowed themselves to be their authentic selves at all (e.g., someone repressed their sexual orientation or gender identity altogether). Moreover, during the 1980s and 1990s, the HIV/AIDS epidemic emerged, and many LGBTQ people witnessed their friends getting sick and dying of a slow, painful disease. Again, maybe addressing microaggressions was not deemed important when LGBTQ people were struggling to even live.

Perhaps 2007 was the right time to reintroduce the concept of microaggressions. During this time, Senator Barack Obama and Senator Hillary Clinton were both running for president of the United States. As people considered the possibility of our country being led by either a Black man or a White woman, racism and sexism became hot topics again. So, when D. W. Sue et al. (2007) reintroduced the concept of microaggressions, a spectrum of research articles and theories emerged, changing the ways discrimination would be discussed in the United States.

MICROAGGRESSION THEORY

Microaggression theory is a model of understanding modern and subtle discrimination in the United States and throughout the world (D. W. Sue, 2010a, 2010b). Although microaggression theory originally centered on perspectives regarding racism and communities of color, the theory expanded to include subtle discrimination toward women (Sue & Capodilupo, 2008), religious minority groups (Nadal, Issa, Griffin, Hamit, & Lyons, 2010), people with disabilities (Keller & Galgay, 2010), and LGBTQ people (Nadal, 2013; Nadal, Rivera, & Corpus, 2010). Although microaggression theory is similar to minority stress theory (Meyer, 1995) and critical race theory (Crenshaw, Gotanda, Peller, & Thomas, 1995), microaggression theory is unique in two major ways. First, previous researchers identified four psychological dilemmas that arise from encounters with microaggressions (D. W. Sue, 2010a, 2010b). Second, microaggression theorists conceptualized three major classifications of microaggressions: microassaults, microinsults, and microinvalidations. D. W. Sue et al. (2007) conceptualized these three manifestations for people of color, and Nadal (2013) applied these concepts to LGBTQ people. I first describe these four psychological dilemmas that sometimes manifest when microaggressions occur, and I then discuss the three main categories of microaggressions.

The Psychological Dilemmas of Microaggressions

The first of four possible dynamics, or psychological dilemmas, that make microaggressions so difficult to discuss or address is *clash of realities*, which describes the conflict that arises when people interpret situations differently. Although perpetrators of microaggressions presume that their behaviors are innocuous or well-intentioned, targets of microaggressions perceive perpetrators' behaviors as biased or malicious. Because of the stark differences in perspectives, it is difficult for people to empathize or communicate with the other without being defensive. For instance, imagine a female supervisor who identifies as a heterosexual ally but occasionally uses subtle, homophobic language around a queer male employee (e.g., substituting the word *heterosexual* with *normal*). The supervisor might not realize she is saying anything offensive unless the employee points it out, and the employee may feel aggravated for always having to do so. If the employee does confront his supervisor on the perceived microaggression, she might feel attacked or hurt or may irately tell him he is too sensitive. Because she cannot understand his perspectives, he may learn to never confront her behavior again.

The second dilemma, *invisibility of unintentional bias,* refers to the idea that people are socialized with dominant group norms and beliefs, which results in implicit bias toward various marginalized groups. For instance, many able-bodied people often do not realize how certain buildings or spaces are not accessible for people with physical disabilities, because they have the privilege of never having to worry about accessibility. Relatedly, people who believe they are equitable may have an especially difficult time in admitting to having any bias. When a person confronts them on a micro-aggression, they might react with various defense mechanisms, including denial, rationalization, or overcompensation. For instance, when the aforementioned employee confronts his supervisor on her microaggressive behaviors, her defense mechanisms can include denial (e.g., "There's no way I have any homophobic biases!"), rationalization (e.g., "It's not my fault I say those things; this is how I was raised!"), or overcompensation (e.g., the day after being confronted, she shows pictures of her gay friends' weddings to her coworkers).

Perceived minimal harm of microaggressions, the third psychological dilemma, refers to the false notion that the impact of microaggressions is minimal and such experiences do not cause much grief or damage in people's lives. Despite many studies supporting the relationship between microaggressions and negative mental health outcomes (Nadal, Whitman, Davis, Erazo, & Davidoff, 2016; Wong, Derthick, David, Saw, & Okazaki, 2014), some people believe those who perceive microaggressions are weak or oversensitive, with one author even calling the concept "pure nonsense" (Thomas, 2008, p. 274).

The fourth psychological dilemma, *catch-22 of responding to microaggressions,* involves the difficulty in addressing microaggressions, especially given the possible consequences. For instance, when experiencing a micro-aggression, someone may not want to reply or challenge the perpetrator because of a lack of time or energy needed to address the microaggression, or because she or he may believe that the perpetrator would be defensive or unreceptive. Safety can determine whether someone would respond to a microaggression (e.g., a woman or LGBTQ person might not respond to verbal harassment when alone and in a public space at night). Context is also a factor of whether to respond (e.g., confronting a supervisor might hurt one's chances for a promotion).

Classifications of Microaggressions

In addition to these psychological dilemmas, microaggression theorists conceptualize three major classifications of microaggressions: microassaults, microinsults, and microinvalidations (D. W. Sue, 2010a, 2010b). D. W. Sue et al. (2007) originally conceptualized these three manifestations of microaggressions for people of color; Nadal (2013) applied these concepts to LGBTQ people. *Microassaults* are verbal or nonverbal insults and behaviors that are typically overt and conscious, mirroring "old-fashioned" discrimination. For instance, in 2015, Donald Trump referred to Mexicans as "lazy" and "rapists" and expressed the sentiment that Muslims should be banned from the United States. Both examples are microassaults because he was deliberate and unapologetic while maintaining he was not racist. Some microassaults might not be malicious in intent but can still convey an individual's conscious or implicit biases. For example, many stand-up comedians, celebrities, or media figures have made stereotypical comments or jokes about a group of people, which often results in a public uproar via social media. Sometimes perpetrators of microaggressions apologize and even assert that they are not prejudiced. In 2013, when Chef Paula Deen's former employees sued her for using the "N word" and creating a racially hostile work environment, Deen apologized publicly and claimed to not be a racist.

Microinsults are interactions that convey stereotypes about people of various groups and typically manifest behaviorally or verbally. Behavioral microinsults range from a person who gawks at a same-sex couple holding hands to a store clerk who follows around a Black or Latino man in a store. A verbal microinsult can include everything from an individual fervently and repeatedly asking an Asian American, "Where are you *really* from?" to an able-bodied person who speaks exceptionally slowly, loudly, or patronizingly to a person who uses a wheelchair for mobility. In each of these examples, a clear insulting or biased message is conveyed: (a) being gay is weird or gross; (b) Black and Latino men are criminal; (c) Asians are not really Americans; and (d) people with disabilities are unintelligent, helpless, or childlike.

Finally, *microinvalidations* are verbal communications that dismiss, refute, or undermine the lived experiences of people of various marginalized groups. Microinvalidations can include situations in which women are told their perceptions of sexism are unsubstantiated or irrational, or people of color are told that they need to stop complaining about racism. In both examples, the microaggression perpetrators assume that their perspective is the only possibility—thus invalidating the target's perspective and reality. People of historically dominant groups (e.g., White people, men, people who are able-bodied) are sometimes unable to empathize with or fully comprehend the realities of people of marginalized groups because their perspectives are so disparate. For instance, imagine a White man who tells a woman of color that she is "too sensitive" or "angry" and passionately claims that racism and sexism do not exist. Because he has never been the target of racism or sexism, he simply cannot grasp her perspectives, let alone empathize with her. Because of his privileged worldview, he believes his perspective is the norm and therefore all other perspectives are insignificant, erroneous, or preposterous.

A REVIEW OF MICROAGGRESSION RESEARCH

Before I review research on how microaggressions manifest in people's lives, I briefly review the previous literature on the influence of discrimination and physical and mental health outcomes. First, research has continually supported that historically marginalized groups face multiple health disparities that make them susceptible for lower quality of life, disabilities, and even premature death (National Institutes of Health, 2010). Communities of color tend to experience a disproportionate prevalence of physical health issues (e.g., cardiovascular disease, diabetes), behavioral health issues (e.g., substance use, cigarette smoking), and mental health issues (e.g., depression, trauma), with multiple studies citing racial discrimination as a major predictor of these problems (see Braveman et al., 2011, for a review). LGBTQ people also disproportionately report mental health issues (e.g., depression, suicide, trauma), behavioral health issues (e.g., substance abuse disorders, risky sexual behaviors), HIV/AIDS, and access to health care; multiple studies have also supported that heterosexist and transphobic discrimination are predictors for poorer health (see Fredriksen-Goldsen et al., 2014, for a review).

Since 2007, more than 100 studies have examined microaggressions with communities of color (see Wong et al., 2014, for a review) and LGBTQ people (see Nadal et al., 2016, for a review). Specifically, studies have examined perspectives of African Americans (D. W. Sue & Capodilupo, 2008; D. W. Sue, Nadal, et al., 2008), Asian Americans (D. W. Sue, Bucceri, Lin, Nadal, & Torino, 2009), Filipino Americans (Nadal, Vigilia Escobar, et al., 2012), Latina/os (Rivera, Forquer, & Rangel, 2010; Torres & Taknint, 2015), multiracial people (Nadal, Wong, et al., 2011), women (Capodilupo et al., 2010; Owen, Tao, & Rodolfa, 2010), LGBQ people (Nadal, Issa, et al., 2011), transgender people (Nadal, Skolnik, & Wong, 2012), people with disabilities (Keller & Galgay, 2010), and Muslims (Nadal, Griffin, et al., 2012). These studies (which use qualitative, quantitative, and mixed methodologies) reveal that people from these various groups are able to identify microaggressions that occur in their lives. In qualitative studies, in particular, participants were able to highlight detailed stories of encounters with microaggressions, as well as recollections of emotions they felt in the short term and long term. So, although naysayers may reject the existence of microaggressions, people from various marginalized groups experience them, identify them as discrimination, and are affected by such encounters in negative ways.

Further, Nadal, Davidoff, et al. (2015) examined the notion of *intersectional microaggressions*—or microaggressions that occur because of individuals' multiple identities. Because people's different identity groups are omnipresent and integrated into how others perceive them, an individual's identity groups (actual or perceived) may influence her or his cumulative experience with microaggressions. For instance, when a woman of color feels isolated or belittled by her coworkers (and perceives those behaviors as microaggressions), the treatment may be due to her race, her gender, both, or a combination with other identities.

Research has shown that microaggressions are predictors of an array of mental outcomes, including traumatic symptoms (Torres & Taknint, 2015), depressive symptoms (Nadal, Griffin, Wong, Hamit, & Rasmus, 2014), suicide (O'Keefe, Wingate, Cole, Hollingsworth, & Tucker, 2015), suicidal ideation (O'Keefe et al., 2015), lower self-esteem (Nadal, Wong,

Griffin, Davidoff, & Sriken, 2014), lower levels of psychological well-being (Nadal, Wong, Sriken, Griffin, & Fujii-Doe, 2015), anxiety and binge drinking (Blume, Lovato, Thyken, & Denny, 2012), and emotional intensity (Wang, Leu, & Shoda, 2011). Given these outcomes, it is evident that microaggressions negatively affect people's lives and need to be studied further.

CASE STUDY

Steven was a 42-year-old, heterosexual, African American man who sought therapy to discuss his anxiety regarding his career. As an assistant professor, he was up for tenure and promotion at the university where he has worked for 6 years. Although hesitant to seek therapy, Steven agreed to it because his wife, Karla, 39, worried he was depressed. In wanting only to work with a psychotherapist of color, Steven found Dr. Whitney Lewis—a Black female counseling psychologist with whom he has been meeting weekly for the past 3 months.

Through initial meetings with Steven, Dr. Lewis learned that he was born in the Southern United States and was the oldest of three children of a working-class family. His parents, James and Katherine, met and married shortly after they graduated from high school. Before retiring, James worked as an auto mechanic and Katherine was an elementary school teacher. His siblings, Damon and Susan, are, respectively, 3 and 5 years younger than Steven. Damon is currently working as a corporate executive and Susan as a dentist. The family originally lived in a rural town in the Southern United States that had a majority-Black population. His parents were heavily active in the Baptist church, and Steven had a large group of friends whom he had known since he was a toddler.

When Steven was 12 years old, his family relocated to a suburban town in the Northeastern United States, where both of his parents were able to find higher paying jobs. Although Steven liked that he lived in a nicer house, the town was almost exclusively White. On his first day of sixth grade, some classmates laughed when Steven was introduced to the class, which made him feel paranoid right away. Later that week, some kids teased Steven about his skin, stating that his dark complexion meant that he was dirty and needed a bath. A week or so later, his classmates referred to him as a monkey and started making "ape sounds" when he walked by them. Whenever these types of incidents occurred, Steven tried to pretend that he was not bothered, although secretly he was extremely distressed and humiliated.

For the rest of the school year, Steven continued to be bullied or ignored. Sometimes the harassment was explicitly race-related (e.g., the bullies made comments about Steven's physical appearance), whereas other times the harassment was not overtly race-based (e.g., they teased Steven about something more innocuous, such as his clothes). Other times, they excluded Steven altogether, never inviting him to join group activities and never picking him for their team during gym class. He never told his teachers, in fear that it would make the situation worse; he never said anything to his parents because he did not want to burden them (and because he was ashamed). So, instead, Steven decided to concentrate on his schoolwork, rationalizing that if he could not be the most popular student, he would be the smartest. Plus, because his classmates had negative stereotypes about Black people, he wanted to prove that he was smarter than them.

When Steven started high school, the harassment from his peers seemed to dwindle. He assumed it was because he stood out less—the high school was much larger than his middle school, and a handful of other students of color attended the school. In his freshman year, he managed to make a few friends with the other honors students in his class. He joined a few clubs and was determined to get into a good college. Every so often, Steven's middle school classmates would revert to making ape noises as he walked down the hallway. Although he was mortified and felt hopeless because the bullying never seemed to go away, he was just relieved that the harassment was not a daily experience anymore.

One day during his junior year of high school, Steven was having a bad day, after receiving a bad grade on his chemistry test. As he left his classroom and walked down the hallway, a classmate began to make those dreaded "ape" noises. Steven reached his breaking point and heatedly ran up to the other student and punched him in the face. A fight ensued, and both students were brought to the principal's office. However, because Steven was the one who threw the first punch, he was suspended for 3 days. When his parents asked about what happened, Steven explosively yelled, "I don't know!" and locked himself in his room. The next day, his parents tried to talk to him, but Steven could not tell them he had been bullied for years.

After Steven graduated from high school, he enrolled in a historically Black university hundreds of miles away. Through his classes and involvement with the Black Student Union, he learned about the history of racism and developed a strong sense of Black identity. He received his bachelor's degree in sociology and began working as a coordinator for a mentoring program for youth of color at a nonprofit organization for several years. Although he liked his job, Steven wanted to do more to advocate for social justice. He decided to pursue his PhD in sociology, with an interest in studying the history of racism and its influence on the educational system.

While in graduate school, Steven met Karla, a Black, Haitian American graduate student who was studying to become a teacher. He was attracted to Karla for her physical beauty, as well as for her knowledge and passion for social justice and education. As they continued to date and become more committed to each other, Steven trusted her and shared his history of bullying and discrimination. Karla was very understanding and shared her own encounters with racism. At that moment, Steven felt very connected to her and knew that she was "the one." A year later, he proposed to her, and they were married a few months after Steven received his doctorate.

Six years ago, Steven was hired at a public university in the sociology department. Although he generally liked the campus where he was employed, he also struggled with being the only Black professor (and one of two professors of color) in his department. Interpersonally, Steven had difficulty maintaining cordial relationships with his colleagues and easily got frustrated with them. One disagreement with one of his White colleagues led to a screaming match between the two of them—which resulted in a stereotype that Steven was "angry" or had "a temper problem," while Steven's White colleague did not suffer any social consequences. Nonetheless, Steven has been quite anxious and despondent about the whole encounter, predominantly since he was being considered for tenure and promotion.

Steven went to therapy because Karla told him she was concerned that he seemed sad and "zoned out" a lot of the time. She thought that it would be a good idea for him to finally confront the demons of his past.

Steven agreed to go to therapy, even though he did not think that there was much to talk about. When Steven first met Dr. Lewis, he discussed his wife's concern about his mood, which he attributed to his anxiety about the tenure process.

Over the next several months in psychotherapy, Dr. Lewis guided Steven in using a race-based trauma approach (Bryant-Davis & Ocampo, 2006). In the first phase, *acknowledgment*, she told Steven that his experiences were real and sadly common for many people of color in the United States. Although Steven knew this to be true, he felt very validated that an outsider recognized this. In the second phase, *sharing*, Dr. Lewis encouraged Steven to recall his past instances with discrimination and encouraged him to disclose these experiences to his wife, too. Steven admitted that White men easily trigger his anger, primarily when he feels like he is being treated as an inferior. In the third phase, *safety and self-care*, Dr. Lewis assessed Steven's coping mechanisms, discussing how safe he felt in various parts of his life. He reported not feeling physically threatened at work but feeling tense every time he had to go to his office (especially to staff meetings). From there, they explored healthy strategies for managing those tensions, including breathing exercises and guided imagery. Steven initially thought these were silly, but he tried them out, practiced them regularly, and saw some usefulness in them.

Now in their fourth month of therapy, Dr. Lewis is working with Steven on grieving or mourning the losses associated with trauma. In this stage, Steven has been connecting to his anger issues, as well as his sadness. He has felt humiliated and resentful that he had been bullied continually throughout his youth; he expressed that he felt like his childhood had been taken away from him. Dr. Lewis has used psychodynamic and Gestalt techniques to assist Steven. In a session, she invited him to participate in an empty-chair exercise in which she asked Steven to imagine that his 12-year-old self was sitting in another chair in the office. Steven thought the exercise was foolish and did not want to attempt it. After unsuccessfully encouraging him to do so, Dr. Lewis decided to ask him to write a letter to his 12-year-old self. He agreed that he would feel more comfortable with this. After writing tearfully for 5 minutes or so, Steven said he was done. Dr. Lewis asked if he might be able to read it aloud, and he agreed.

Steven connected with his sadness in a way that he reported he had not done in decades.

CASE STUDY DISCUSSION AND CLINICAL RECOMMENDATIONS

In reviewing the case of Steven, the first of many elements to consider is that he clearly had faced both overt discrimination (e.g., being referred to as a monkey) and microaggressions (e.g., being stereotyped as an angry Black man, while his White colleague did not experience any negative consequences). Although most of the bullying Steven endured during adolescence could be considered overtly racist, some of the bullying could fit the definition of microassault or microinsult. For instance, the isolation Steven felt when his classmates never invited him to join in any activities might be interpreted as a response to a microinsult. Without explicitly saying they were isolating him because of his race, Steven could infer his "otherness" was the cause for this exclusion. However, because he could not definitively say this was the reason, he may doubt himself and internalize negative feelings. Further, much of the bullying might possibly be interpreted as a microassault, depending on the boys' rationales. If the boys admitted they were being racist, the behavior could clearly be labeled as overt racism. Yet, if the boys denied that race had anything to do with their mistreatment (e.g., they picked on him because he was the "new kid" and not because of race), this could be viewed as a microassault.

Second, Steven's case exemplifies how traumatic discrimination (particularly during one's formative years) can have profound effects on people's entire lives. Steven experienced severe psychological consequences as a young person, and he repressed a lot of negative emotions, likely because he suffered in silence and never disclosed these experiences to anyone. Decades later, these past traumas still affect his life. In fact, he admitted to being easily agitated by his White colleagues, who he said make him feel "belittled or inferior." Through therapy, Steven recognized that although his colleagues' behavior was indeed microaggressive and problematic, his interactions with them were mere triggers. When he lost his temper with them, he was not only reacting to present-day incidents but also responding to the traumatic events he had never healed from. In this way, Steven's current encounters with microaggressions were both triggering and retraumatizing.

Finally, it is necessary to recognize the ways in which racial identity may influence Steven's worldviews. *Racial identity* is the extent to which a person feels most connected to individuals of their own race, as well as how they feel about themselves, their own race, and other racial groups (Helms, 1995). Because Steven spent his early childhood among other Black Americans, he experienced a culture shock when his family relocated to a predominantly White neighborhood. As the only Black student, he felt isolated, which may have contributed to negative feelings about his race and himself. Given his negative encounters with race during this time, it is possible he had developed feelings of *internalized racism,* that is, the notion that a person of color learns and retains negative beliefs and stereotypes about her or his own group. Similarly, the concept of *internalized oppression,* or being socialized to maintain adverse and harmful beliefs about one's self or group, can be applied to many other historically marginalized groups (e.g., women, LGBTQ people; see David, 2014, for a review).

Finally, it appears that Steven purposefully sought a historically Black university so that he could finally be surrounded by people who were similar to him and learn more about the history of racism toward Black people in the United States. Some people may argue Steven had developed an ethnocentric identity, in that he appeared to prefer to be in the company of Black people and even preferred a Black therapist. Conversely, others might argue he had an integrated sense of identity, in that he preferred to have friends (and a therapist) who he believed he would not have to explain much to and who could potentially validate his experiences with, and perspectives about, race and racism.

3

Racial Microaggressions and Trauma

R ace (a socially constructed system of classifying people on the basis of their skin color, physical features, and hair texture) is an integral part of American society. Historically, race has been used to uplift and privilege White Americans, while marginalizing and degrading Native Americans, Black Americans, Asian Americans, Pacific Islanders, Latina/os, Arab Americans, and multiracial people. To understand the relationship between race, discrimination, and trauma, the chapter reviews the context of racism in the United States, as well as the previous theoretical and empirical literature on racial microaggressions, and its influence on trauma.

http://dx.doi.org/10.1037/0000073-004
Microaggressions and Traumatic Stress: Theory, Research, and Clinical Treatment, by K. L. Nadal

THE 2008 PRESIDENTIAL ELECTION
AND THE CHANGING FACE OF RACISM

When Barack Obama was first elected president of the United States in 2008, there were both positive and negative reactions around the country and across the world. First, many Americans were genuinely hopeful. With two terms under President George W. Bush, the economy had plummeted, the country was recovering after spending millions on the war with Iraq, and the general morale of the American people was low. Senator Barack Obama was a visionary with ideas and strategies for turning the country around. He inspired young people to care about their government and encouraged older people to become reinvested in the country. To many people, he represented what the United States needed—a young, motivated, and fresh leader who did not come from a long legacy of politicians and who was free of any political scandal. His intellect, charisma, and seemingly sincere demeanor were refreshing during a time when many people in society felt that they had no voice in how their country was governed.

Second, many Americans vocalized their feelings of pride that the United States had, for the first time in history, elected a person of color to become the Commander-in-Chief. Black Americans and many other people of color were particularly moved by this election because many never expected that a person of color would ever be able to hold this position of power—at least not in their lifetimes. Given the history of racism in the United States, especially slavery and civil injustices against Black Americans, as well as people's own experiences with racial discrimination, many people of color had developed the worldview that racism was omnipresent and that White people would always hold the ultimate power in the United States. So, when President Obama was elected in 2008, many Americans, including those who had lost hope in democracy, reported a spectrum of emotions, including joy, amazement, optimism, and triumph.

However, some people responded to President Obama's election with disapproval and even hate. In December 2008, *The Huffington Post* compiled a sampling of the racial incidents that took place after the presidential election (Mitchell, 2008), including the following:

- A Maine convenience store displayed a sign called "The Osama Obama Shotgun Pool," which invited customers to place bets on when they thought President Obama would be assassinated. The sign also read, "Let's hope we have a winner."
- In North Carolina, four college students were accused of spray painting "Kill that nigger" and "Shoot Obama" at the North Carolina State University's free expression tunnel.

Although these incidents (and others) did not lead to court cases or convictions, these types of reported incidents demonstrate that many Americans rejected the election of a Black president and overtly enacted their racial biases as a result.

A final response to President Obama's election was the belief that there was a shift in how meritocracy operated in the United States. Although President Obama was the son of a working-class White single mother from Kansas and an absent Black father from Kenya, he managed to achieve the most powerful position in the country. With few resources, he was admitted to Columbia University, where he earned a bachelor's degree in political science, and was later admitted into Harvard Law School, where he earned his JD. After becoming the first Black student to be elected as president of the *Harvard Law Review*, he later became a community organizer, a civil rights attorney, a lecturer at the University of Chicago Law School, a senator from Illinois, and eventually president of the United States. If a Black, biracial child of a single-parent family could be elected president, perhaps opportunities were equal for all and anyone could achieve their dreams.

It was also during this time that many journalists and news pundits began to label President Obama's election as the beginning of a *post-racial era*. The term, which was first coined in 1971 in *The New York Times*, connotes that many people believe that racial discrimination is a concept of the past and that racism no longer exists in American society

(Wooten, 1971). Many media personalities made comments about the United States entering this alleged postracial era, including radio host Lou Dobbs, who in November 2009 said, "We are now in a 21st-century post-partisan, post-racial society" (Dawson & Bobo, 2009, p. 247). Major newspapers (including *The Wall Street Journal, The New York Times,* and *The Boston Globe*) cited this "postracial" sentiment as well. MSNBC host Chris Matthews even claimed, "[President Obama] is post-racial by all appearances. You know, I forgot he was Black tonight for an hour" (Omni & Winant, 2014, p. 2). Although Matthews's comment was likely well-intentioned, it actually is reflective of his implicit bias and covert racism: Because the newly elected president did not fit Matthews's schema of Black people, he was deemed to have no race—or, more likely, to seem White.

Although the term was used more frequently after the 2008 election, the concept of "postracial" had been written about in prior academic contexts for at least a decade. Instead of "postracial," psychology scholars referred to this paradigm as "colorblindness," or the belief that "race *should* not and *does* not matter" (Neville, Lilly, Duran, Lee, & Browne, 2000, p. 60). At first glance, the definition might not seem like a horrid concept, particularly because believing that race should not matter speaks to an individual's belief in equity and fairness regardless of one's race. People who think that race should not matter likely believe people should not be treated differently or that people of different racial groups should not be denied access to opportunities, resources, or access to the American dream. However, the colorblind notion that race does not matter is problematic for a few reasons. First, believing that race does not matter is inaccurate, because it does: Research supports that systemic racism does exist, as evidenced by racial disparities in economics, educational outcomes, incarceration rates, hate violence incidents, prevalence of deaths by police, and many others (Neville, Gallardo, & Sue, 2016). Research also shows that interpersonal racism exists as well, as evidenced by the 40 years of research studies that document people of color's experiences with racial discrimination and its influence on physical and mental health (Nadal, 2011; Nadal, Griffin, Wong, Hamit, & Rasmus, 2014; D.W. Sue et al., 2007). Because racism does, in fact, exist, telling someone that race does not matter negates and invalidates the racial realities of people of color, who face racism every day of their lives. So, although some people may want to believe that President Obama's election symbolized the end of racism, too much empirical evidence demonstrates that racism is omnipresent and far from over in American society.

These reactions to President Obama's election and presidency exemplify the different types of racial biases and attitudes that American people maintain. First, some people still consciously hold onto racial biases, sometimes enacting these biases through hate crimes and other discriminatory behaviors. Despite this, being overtly racist is not favorable in the majority of contemporary American society, not only because of hate crime legislation and antidiscrimination laws but also because of general society norms. Thus, even if people hold onto racial biases, they tend not to be vocal (particularly in public spaces or in workplaces), as such biases may have dire consequences (e.g., some White people who openly participated in a White nationalist rally in Charlottesville, Virginia in August 2017 were fired from their jobs). Instead, overtly racist people tend to be more private (e.g., sharing opinions with loved ones with similar views) or anonymous in vocalizing their beliefs (e.g., anonymously writing in online comments sections).

Second, individuals who do not engage in overtly racist acts may ostracize those individuals who do, thereby distancing themselves from any potential biases or behaviors. For instance, many White Americans view themselves as "good people" while viewing White supremacists, or White nationalist, as being the "real" racists. In these instances, many White people are not able to articulate the racial biases that they have learned, have been socialized with, or still maintain. As a result, many White people may externalize that racism is a behavior that is perpetuated by others, thereby freeing themselves from any potential guilt of or responsibility for personal racial bias or discrimination. Further, because of this dynamic, White people tend to be more defensive when challenged on their privilege: Because they are not prejudiced (at least not consciously), they do not want to be labeled in the same category as White supremacists or bigots.

Third, some people may believe that race should no longer matter in our society and aim to be colorblind. These individuals insist that others should be treated fairly and that individuals should be judged for their merits and personality traits, rather than for the color of their skin. Sometimes these individuals insist that if a person works hard enough, they can accomplish their goals, regardless of their race. They sometimes deny that certain people or groups have disadvantages, citing that there is an "equal playing field" for everyone. These individuals also claim to be "good people" and likely have difficulty in recognizing their own racial biases too.

One vivid illustration of how colorblindness has manifested in the present-day United States became apparent shortly after the #BlackLivesMatter campaign took off in late 2012 to recognize the disproportionate number of Black Americans (particularly men) who had been killed in the United States—by civilians (e.g., Trayvon Martin), by police officers (e.g., Michael Brown, Eric Garner, Tamir Rice), or in mysterious ways (e.g., Sandra Bland). Most of these cases (and many others) resulted in nonconvictions. The creators of #BlackLivesMatter aimed to call attention to the fact that Black lives *need to* matter in the United States, and that for this to happen, Americans needed to proclaim that Black lives *do* matter.

Many people, mostly White, were publicly outraged by this campaign and began a counter hashtag #AllLivesMatter—signifying that they believed that society should care about the lives of all people. Many people agreed with this revised message of #AllLivesMatter because it inclusively states that *every* life should be valued in this country (and across the world). However, their assertion that the #BlackLivesMatter campaign should be modified to include "all" people demonstrates a few key notions of White privilege and colorblindness. First, because many White people (and others) are so uncomfortable with recognizing systemic racism and their own potential benefits of racism, they are unable to hear the intentions and meanings of the #BlackLivesMatter movement. Leaders and supporters of #BlackLivesMatter (which consists of Black people, other people of color, and socially conscious White people) had never insinuated that Black lives are the *only* ones that matter (or that society should disregard non-Black lives). Instead, the message was that Black lives *need to* matter *right now*. By suggesting otherwise,

#AllLivesMatter proponents deny the reality of systemic racism and ignore decades of research indicating that Black men are killed by police at disproportionate rates. Plus, the fact many White people wanted to override or subdue #BlackLivesMatter demonstrated the need to dominate or deny perspectives that did not match their own. Instead of allowing for activists of color to speak their minds and share their perspectives, #AllLivesMatter supporters needed to inform them that their racial and political views were wrong or invalid.

Given these various perspectives, particularly those of well-intentioned White people and those individuals who aim to be colorblind, there are so many reasons why people, especially White people, may have difficulty recognizing that microaggressions do exist in people's lives. If they were to acknowledge that microaggressions or any type of discrimination occurs, they might have to also acknowledge that they indeed have some subtle or unconscious racial bias that results in their own perpetuating of racial microaggressions. Second, they would have to admit that the world was not as equitable a place as they believed it to be—forcing them to (a) confront the privileges that they do not recognize or that they try to deny and (b) acknowledge the injustice that others, namely, people of color, face in their everyday lives.

Regardless of the possible explanations for denying racism and racial microaggressions in the world, it is quite difficult and distressing for people (specifically White people) to talk about race and racism. In general, White Americans believe it is impolite or socially awkward to discuss issues of race with people of color and even with each other. Researchers have described this concept as "difficult dialogues," or challenging and stressful conversations about issues of multiculturalism, diversity, power, and privilege (D. W. Sue, Lin, Torino, Capodilupo, & Rivera, 2009). White people may not want to talk about race with people of color because they do not want to offend anyone and "say the wrong thing" (and thereby look biased or racist). Conversely, White people may not like talking about race with other White people either—perhaps due to the social norms of middle-class White families that teach one to avoid topics of race, religion, and politics, or because acknowledging their privilege and their benefits from systemic racism is uncomfortable.

REVIEW OF RACIAL MICROAGGRESSIONS LITERATURE

Nearly thirty years after Pierce et al.'s (1978) original conceptualizations of racial microaggressions, D. W. Sue et al. (2007) proposed a theoretical taxonomy to describe the many types of racial microaggressions faced by people of color, citing an array of themes, including

- *criminality/assumption of criminality:* instances in which people of color, particularly Black and Latina/o/x Americans, are presumed to be dangerous or criminally deviant (e.g., a White woman grips her purse when a Black man enters an elevator);
- *alien in one's own land:* instances in which people of color may be treated like perpetual foreigners (e.g., presuming that an Asian American would not speak English and complimenting her or him on not having an accent);
- *second-class citizen:* instances in which people of color encounter second-rate assistance or treatment in comparison with White people (e.g., a Latina woman who is continually passed over for a leadership position, despite her seniority or productivity);
- *ascription of intelligence:* instances in which people of color are stereotypically appraised for their level of intellect, aptitude, or leadership (e.g., a White professor presumes that a Black male student must be on an athletic scholarship; a supervisor assigns an Asian American a math-related task); and
- *colorblindness:* instances in which White people tell people of color that race or racism does not exist or is unimportant (e.g., a White man tells a woman of color that he "does see not her race" and that "he only sees her").

For the next several years, the proposed themes in this taxonomy were explored and validated through an array of qualitative studies, most of which used focus group methodologies and asked people about their experiences with microaggressions. These earlier studies shared views from participants who identified as Black Americans, Latinas/Latinos, Asian Americans, indigenous people, multiracial people, Filipino Americans, and students of color in general (see Nadal, Griffin, et al., 2014, for a review). The themes that emerged were used to create a measure on racial microaggressions—the Racial and Ethnic Microaggression Scale (see Nadal, 2011). Studies revealed racial microaggressions predicted self-esteem scores for college students of color (Nadal, Wong, Griffin, Davidoff, & Sriken, 2014), and other studies demonstrated how a larger accumulation of racial microaggressions resulted in both depressive symptoms and a negative perspective of the world (Nadal, Griffin, et al., 2014). Another study found that when Latina/o/x and Asian Americans encountered microaggressions, they were also likely to report symptoms of anxiety, anger, and stress, (Huynh, 2012). Studies have demonstrated how racial microaggressions negatively affect workplace climate for people of color—Black faculty members report being treated differently than White faculty (Cartwright, Washington, & McConnell, 2009), and Asian Americans are less likely than White people to be hired for jobs that require social skills (Lai & Babcock, 2013).

Further, Torres and Taknint (2015) proposed a mediational model to examine the relationship between ethnic identity, self-efficacy, traumatic stress, and racial microaggressions. With a sample of 113 Latina/o/x adults, results indicated that when Latina/o/x people encounter racial microaggressions, they are likely to report traumatic symptoms, which may also result in depressive symptoms. The study also found that ethnic identity and self-efficacy were moderators between microaggressions and traumatic stress. In other words, when people have stronger levels of ethnic identity (e.g., pride, connection to one's ethnic group) and self-efficacy (e.g., ability to function and succeed), they might be less likely to develop symptoms of trauma, even when encountering microaggressions. Thus, if people of color feel good about themselves and their ethnic groups, they might be better able to cope with racial microaggressions, which may protect them from experiencing symptoms related to trauma and depression.

CASE STUDY

Liz was a 21-year-old college student who was referred to the University Counseling Center at Midwestern University (a pseudonym) by Dr. Andrea Nelson, director of the Multicultural Center. Dr. Nelson informed the staff that Liz, who was a well-known student leader on campus, had had a public, explosive meltdown in the lobby of her center. According to many students, Liz began screaming, crying, and angrily yelling "None of you understand!" She then ran into a room at the Multicultural Center, where she sobbed loudly in the dark for 15 minutes. One of the students informed Dr. Nelson—who found Liz in the fetal position on the floor, bawling boisterously and uncontrollably. After about an hour of talking, Dr. Nelson convinced Liz to accompany her to the Counseling Center to talk to one of the staff psychologists.

In her intake session, Liz informed the psychologist that she identified as a queer, multiracial person of color of Dominican, Sioux, and Black heritage. She was the only child of her parents, and she grew up in an upper-middle-class neighborhood in a liberal metropolitan city. Liz described finding solace in the Multicultural Center on campus (as well as the Black, Latina/o/x, and Native American student organizations) because there were so few people of color on campus. Although she identified as queer, she was not involved in the lesbian, gay, bisexual, transgender, and queer student organization, as she found the group to be "pretty White" and not aligned with her social justice values.

When asked about the incident at the Multicultural Center, Liz revealed she had been extremely distressed because of the aftermath of some student protests she had been leading on campus. She described how she learned about a White fraternity that hosted a racial theme party on campus. The fraternity advertised a "ghetto" themed party and that everyone should dress as their favorite "hip-hop thug or gangster." Liz and a few other student leaders decided to attend the party. When one of the fraternity members opened the door, Liz was outraged and disgusted to see that he was dressed in a hooded sweatshirt, gold chains, and foundation makeup on his face that was darker than the rest of his body. When she demanded that he let them in, he refused, stating that it was a private party and he did not want them to "ruin the vibe." Liz started to yell at him and several other partygoers who were near the door; she took photos on her cell phone before they slammed the door on the group of students of color.

Distraught and amped up, Liz decided to post the pictures on her social media wall and wrote about her experience at the fraternity house. Her post was forwarded to the editor of the campus newspaper, who asked Liz if they were going to take any action or file any complaints. Liz informed the editor how multicultural student groups were going to have a sit-in on the campus quad to protest the incident and all the other institutionalized racism on campus. More than 200 students attended the sit-in, holding signs with messages such as "Black Lives Matter," "Revolucíon," and "No More Racism at MU."

That afternoon, in her American History class, Liz's professor was lecturing about the Civil War but did not cover any issues related to slavery or racism during that time. Still distraught by the happenings of the fraternity party and the rally, Liz raised her hand and asked the professor why he did not cover such topics. The professor responded, "When you get a PhD and get to teach a class, you can talk about all of those things." Liz uttered back, "Whoa. White privilege, much?" to which her professor sarcastically replied, "Apparently, everything is racist. Maybe you are too sensitive." Several students in the class laughed, and Liz stormed out of the class. She rushed to her apartment and cried herself to sleep for a few hours.

While checking her phone (which had been silent while she slept), Liz noticed many friends had sent her multiple text messages throughout the night, informing her that the campus newspaper had published an online article about the rally. In the article, the editor referred to Liz as "attention-seeking" and "angry"—stating he did not think that the party was racist and that the whole protest was a "waste of time." He continued to write that if she did not agree with the party, she should not have attended. In the comments section of the online article, several fraternity members started to write hurtful comments about Liz, ridiculing her appearance (e.g., her hair, her body shape, the clothes she was wearing) and posting unflattering photos of her they found on various social media sites. Nonstudents, unrelated to the university, also commented on the article, writing a slew of demeaning remarks about Liz. Although a few of the online comments were positive and supportive of Liz and the other students of color, the majority were hostile, cruel, and disparaging.

Liz was shocked by the article and the comments section. She had thought the editor contacted her because he was in support of the students of color and would write a favorable article. She was also shocked that so many people would be so critical of the protest, because she thought the racially themed party was a clear-cut example of racism. Perhaps the most traumatic aspect of the article was that she did not expect people to attack her personal character or reputation. Liz has always believed she was a good-hearted and kind person; however, the article made her question why she was viewed as "angry" and "attention-seeking."

As Liz opened her laptop to start working on a letter in response to the editor, she opened her e-mail account and found she had more than 100 e-mail messages, all directed to her, from strangers from all over the country. Apparently, the fraternity had posted Liz's student e-mail address on the article's website and encouraged people to e-mail her to share their perspectives about the incident. Liz's heart dropped. She felt like she was in a nightmare and did not know why she was being targeted. As she opened the first e-mail, she saw a five-paragraph tirade written in all capital letters; in the second e-mail, someone had taken a photo from her Facebook page and edited the words "Affirmative Action at MU" across her face. She read a few more hurtful, vindictive, and hostile e-mails before closing her laptop and turning off her phone altogether. She cried herself back to sleep—feeling worthless, edgy, violated, and alone.

For the next 3 days, Liz stayed home from all her classes because she was too embarrassed, scared, and despondent to face the world. She wondered what she had done to deserve this type of treatment. Her roommates knocked on the door to check on her, but she refused to come out, except to use the bathroom and get food. She brushed her teeth in the morning but did not have any energy to take a shower or wash her face. She had completely forgotten about all her responsibilities, including her midterms, her extracurricular activities, and her friends.

Four days later, one of Liz's closest friends, Nicole, knocked on her apartment door. Nicole had been trying to get in contact with Liz, but because Liz's phone was off, she had no way of reaching her. Fortunately, Nicole had been in touch with Liz's roommates, who informed her they knew that Liz was at home and that she just did not want to talk to anyone. Nicole was worried about Liz and wanted to see whether there was anything she could do for her. When Liz answered the door, Nicole's first reaction was that Liz looked disheveled, edgy, fearful, and zoned out. Nicole tried everything she could to make Liz smile, but she failed miserably;

throughout their conversation, Liz appeared to space out, not hearing or not responding to Nicole's questions. Still hopeful, Nicole asked Liz to go with her to their Black Student Union's social gathering at the Multicultural Center the next day. Nicole told Liz how everyone missed her and how everyone wanted to make sure she was okay. Liz was hesitant in going, but she also realized that she had not left her apartment in 4 days. Plus, she saw that Nicole looked really sad to see her in this state, so, although ambivalent, she agreed.

The next day, Liz finally took a shower and reluctantly left her apartment, without her phone or laptop (neither of which she had touched for days). From her apartment to the Multicultural Center was usually a brisk 5-minute walk, but on this particular day, it seemed to take an eternity. As Liz walked her usual path, she noticed a few students (all White) snickering as she walked by them. She could not tell whether the laughter was all directed toward her or whether they were reacting to someone or something else. She decided to run to the Multicultural Center so she could get there faster. When she saw Nicole, Liz ran up to her and began wailing and screaming uncontrollably.

CASE STUDY DISCUSSION AND CLINICAL RECOMMENDATIONS

Liz's story illustrates multiple concepts that are discussed in this chapter. Before I unpack the story itself, it is crucial to examine Liz's history and racial identity development, which can help with hypothesizing possible reasons she had this "explosive" and tearful breakdown at the Multicultural Center. First, Liz reported that she had never really encountered any racism or discrimination before she attended college, asserting that her hometown was a more liberal environment. Although her perception may be true, it is also necessary to consider that perhaps Liz may have been exposed to some discrimination but may not have perceived it as such. Studies on racial identity development have supported that people of color tend to undergo several statuses of identity development, which scholars suggest can be determined by (a) how they feel about themselves and their racial group, (b) how they may perceive racism and fairness in the world, and (c) how they interact with others of their similar racial group or other racial groups (DeCuir-Gunby, 2009). Perhaps Liz did not ever notice racism because she had not yet dealt with any overtly racist incident; although blatant racism can be sad and distressful, these "awakening" moments can be useful in allowing people to understand the realities of the world (Nadal, 2004). Similarly, perhaps Liz did not recognize racism before because she lived in a protective environment where her parents provided her with access to resources and because many people of color were around her. Either way, when Liz first arrived on campus, she noticed that there were very few students of color, which then made her feel "othered."

Second, Liz had clearly experienced multiple forms of discrimination, ranging from overt harassment to subtler or seemingly innocuous microaggressions. Often, when people face blatant discrimination of any form, they become more attuned or perceptive to more covert forms of discrimination (and vice versa). I first highlight the overt forms of discrimination that Liz encountered. The racially themed fraternity party, which was the original source of conflict, is an example of an overt form of racism in that partygoers were encouraged to dress in modern-day blackface. Racially themed parties are quite common on campuses across the United States and cause multiple stressors for students of color and overall campus morale (Garcia, Johnston, Garibay, Herrera, & Giraldo, 2011). The "ghetto" themed party is just one example of parties that have been reported on college campuses; others include "Mexican night," where party goers dress in stereotypical sombreros, ponchos, and moustaches, and "Oriental night," where guests don clichéd "Asian outfits" and speak with cartoonish Asian accents.

Although some may argue racially themed parties are overtly racist, it might also be argued that such parties would be considered microassaults. When people host or participate in these parties, many do not believe that they are doing anything wrong—often claiming their intention is to "celebrate" the cultural group they are dressed as. Because of this, their intention is not to hurt communities of color but rather to have a good time and to do something that they deem original. Oftentimes, supporters of these types of parties contend it is "just another theme party," in the same way that a toga party celebrates Ancient Greece or Ancient Rome. Because they do not believe they are engaging in any racially biased activity, they have the potential to become defensive and refuse to apologize for their behavior, often characterizing the complainers as oversensitive killjoys. In this way, the themed party does fit the criteria for a micro-assault in that they were conscious of their actions but their intention was not harmful, which differs from old-fashioned, overtly biased forms of discrimination, in which an individual overtly and intentionally wanted to affront or demean another group.

The second form of overt discrimination that Liz encountered was the cyberbullying that occurred after the campus newspaper posted an article about the student protest. *Cyberbullying* is the "willful and repeated harm inflicted [on another] through the use of computers, cell phones, or other electronic devices" (Hinduja & Patchin, 2010, p. 208). Researchers have discussed the ways in which cyberbullying has become more commonplace in the lives of young people and that people who are targeted for cyberbullying experience multiple negative outcomes and are susceptible to multiple mental health issues, including depression, anxiety, substance use, risky sexual behaviors, and even suicide (Rice et al., 2015). Because Liz had gotten involved in student activism and publicly challenged an entire fraternity on their biases, she was an easy target for retaliation. The online bullies wrote hurtful comments on the article, even going out of their way to harass Liz through her personal e-mail address (which was easily found on a campus directory).

Further, through this cyberbullying, Liz's multiple identities, particularly as a woman of color, were being targeted. First, as a woman, Liz was cyberbullied on her appearance—a form of harassment or discrimination that occurs less for men. Given that society is less critical of men's appearances than of women's (e.g., society's messages impart that men can grow older or gain weight and still be viewed as attractive, whereas women who grow older or gain weight are viewed as undesirable and dreadful), these types of messages are especially harmful for women, who are encouraged to reach nearly impossible body ideals. Second, as a woman of color, when her bullies disparage her intellect, it could be because of her race, her gender, or both.

In the scenario, many examples of microaggressions appear to manifest in different forms, driven by multiple types of intentions. For instance, Liz experienced a multitude of racial microinvalidations, including (a) the fraternity member's telling her that he did not want her to "ruin the vibe" of the party; (b) the newspaper editor's calling the student protest "a waste of time"; and (c) the professor's denying her perceptions of racism and telling her that she should not be "so sensitive." Liz also felt some microaggressions that might be more difficult to "prove," which left her feeling confused and slightly paranoid. For instance, when she noticed the stares, laughter, and scoffing, she did not know for certain that the behavior was all intended for her. If she were to confront any of those individuals, they could deny wrongdoing and accuse her of being "angry" and "paranoid," which are two stereotypes that Liz wanted to avoid.

A further note for exploration is the notion of whether people believe that Liz was "asking for it" when she chose to attend the fraternity party. Some people might attest that if she did not attend the party or just kept quiet, she would have never gotten into this predicament to begin with. The concept of presuming that Liz was responsible for the string of discriminatory events that she underwent matches what psychology researchers refer to as *victim blaming*, the notion that some people are unfairly held responsible for their misfortunes. Although victim blaming has likely existed throughout history, it became a topic of interest that initially focused on how women were to be faulted for being targeted for sexual violence. For the past two decades, various research studies have found that victim blaming further contributes to survivors' experiences with trauma, resulting in mental health issues (e.g., anxiety, depression, posttraumatic stress disorder [PTSD]) and difficulties with self-esteem and relationships with others (e.g., self-blame, self-silencing, distrust of others; Harber, Podolski, & Williams, 2015). Specific to racism, one experimental study found that White people tended to blame people of color who cited racial discrimination as a reason for not getting hired for a job (Kaiser & Miller, 2003). In Liz's case, a similar sentiment may be present, that is, even though the fraternity was responsible for hosting a party that many might consider racist, Liz was viewed as "a troublemaker" for confronting the group and staging a peaceful protest. So even though protest is at the core of the values of this country (e.g., the

American Revolution, the Boston Tea Party), when Black people (and other people of color) protest, it is viewed as a nuisance or as problematic.

Finally, although the harassment and subsequent discrimination that Liz experienced might not be considered a "trauma" according to the standards and definitions in the *Diagnostic and Statistical Manual of Mental Disorders* (5th ed.; American Psychiatric Association, 2013), or the *International Classification of Diseases* (10th ed.; World Health Organization, 1992), it is worthwhile to explore whether Liz exhibited any of the criteria related to PTSD or acute stress disorder (ASD). First, the traumatic event seemed to have only have lasted for a few days (as described in this case), indicating that Liz did not (yet) fit the criteria for PTSD, whose diagnosis requires that symptoms have persisted for more 30 days. Instead, the symptoms appeared to have lasted for at least 2 days (but no more than 30 days), which indicates that a diagnosis of ASD might be a better fit. Third, the symptoms would not have been caused by substance use or physiological explanations, which we can presume was the case for Liz. Further, the symptoms must severely affect overall functioning—that was clearly the case with Liz, who had not gone to class for several days and who was having trouble with basic functioning.

An individual who is diagnosed with ASD would have to exhibit at least nine of the 20 criteria associated with PTSD. In reviewing the case (and depending on how much more information we can gather), it can be argued that Liz could undoubtedly fit at least 10 criteria, with a few more that would likely be applicable too. For instance, Liz had recurrent, involuntary, and intrusive recollections of the traumatic event, as indicated by her distressing and ruminating thoughts about the trauma. She also appeared to avoid all trauma-related emotions and external reminders (e.g., she refused to turn on her laptop or mobile phone), and she lost all interest in activities that she enjoyed before the trauma. Her outburst at the Multicultural Center is an example of her trauma-related emotions (e.g., anger, fright, repulsion, guilt, shame). More information is needed, but she likely blamed herself for the incident and felt alienated from others. And from the one experience she had in leaving her apartment, it appears that Liz has become hypervigilant about her surroundings.

The psychologist at the Counseling Center could evaluate Liz for other symptoms that are likely to have some relevance. For example, Liz might be able to share whether she has had any flashbacks or other dissociations. She could reveal whether she was having any disturbances in her sleep or whether her beliefs or expectations about herself or the world have changed (e.g., did Liz think that she was worthless or that the world was no longer a safe place?). Further, it would be important to assess whether Liz continued to have intense or prolonged distress after being exposed to traumatic reminders or whether she had noticeable physiological reactivity after exposure to these triggers. Whatever the outcome of such a psychological evaluation, it is worth noting that if Liz was viewed as being overly dramatic or having bad coping skills (thereby not identified as having experienced trauma), a psychologist or other clinician would not even consider some of these symptoms.

One approach that might be useful in working with Liz is racial trauma recovery (Comas-Díaz, 2016). In the first phase, it may be important to assess the trauma that Liz has experienced and work on stabilizing her symptoms. To do so, a therapist may choose to administer the Race-Based Traumatic Stress Symptom Scale (Carter et al., 2013), which could assist in understanding how severe Liz's symptoms were. When processing her experience with the scale, the therapist should employ humanistic techniques such as empathy, genuineness, and unconditional positive regard, especially because it appears that part of Liz's retraumatizing is that she feels that no one believes her. Once a therapist is able to help Liz to control some of her symptoms, it may be beneficial to assist her with any internalized oppression (e.g., ways that she may actually believe the negative things people are saying about her) and decolonization (i.e., ways to identify, combat, and free herself from the negative messages she has learned as a woman of color), which would hopefully result in her returning to her passion as a student leader and activist. Finally, as Liz begins to heal from the trauma, the therapist might employ "wisdom enhancing" techniques, which may assist Liz in reframing the entire incident as a form of empowerment.

4

Sexual Orientation Microaggressions and Trauma

In this chapter, I review the spectrum of microaggressions that target people on the basis of their sexual orientation. *Sexual orientation* is a person's sense of personal and social identity, which is typically based on three components: (a) who a person is sexually attracted to, (b) the behaviors through which a person expresses or acts upon those sexual attractions, and (c) the sense of belonging to groups or communities who share those identities (Nadal, 2013). The chapter begins with an analysis of the current state of heterosexism in the United States, as well as the extant literature on microaggressions that target lesbian, gay, bisexual, and queer (LGBQ) people. I discuss microaggressions based on gender identity in Chapter 6, as sexual orientation and gender identity are separate constructs that warrant their own examination. Accordingly, *LGBTQ* refers to the general umbrella population, and *LGBQ* specifically connotes the group or groups of individuals who identify as nonheterosexual.

http://dx.doi.org/10.1037/0000073-005
Microaggressions and Traumatic Stress: Theory, Research, and Clinical Treatment, by K. L. Nadal
Copyright © 2018 by the American Psychological Association. All rights reserved.

BEYOND THE U.S. SUPREME COURT DECISIONS: HETEROSEXISM IN THE UNITED STATES

Many Americans believe discrimination no longer exists for histori-cally marginalized groups. For LGBQ people, the first of a few reasons that people might make this assumption is that, in comparison with prior decades, many LGBQ people are living in out, proud, and authentic ways—with many developing healthy sexual and romantic relationships and belonging to communities with others who have shared identities and experiences. Even for those who do not live in LGBQ-populated areas, technology has enabled many LGBQ people to find each other, even when physical safe spaces do not exist.

Perhaps the most telling sign of the increased acceptance of LGBTQ people was the Supreme Court of the United States (SCOTUS) *Obergefell v. Hodges* (2015) decision. With a 5-to-4 majority vote, the court decision officially ended state bans on same-sex marriage, resulting in marriage equality on the federal level. Although a historic case, the decision was part of a series of legislations that granted LGBTQ people rights that pre-viously were not afforded to them. From 2004 to 2015, 37 states passed laws that legalized same-sex marriage. In 2009, President Obama signed a different bill that officially recognized sexual orientation and gender iden-tity as protected classes under federal law, and in 2010, President Obama signed a federal bill allowing LGBQ people to openly serve in the military. One major shift in the social climate was in May 2012, when President Obama publicly shared his support for same-sex marriage. He stated that his position had "evolved" and that he thought it was important for him to affirm that same-sex couples should be able to get married (Calmes & Baker, 2012). As the first sitting president to support marriage equality, President Obama's new perspective likely reflected the general American public's "evolving" sentiments as well. One explanation for this shift is intergroup contact theory, which suggests prejudice is reduced when people have more exposure to others that are different from them (Allport, 1954). When heterosexual people (e.g., President Obama) meet, and form mean-ingful relationships with, LGBQ people, they may learn to be more open-minded and accepting. And when the majority of members of American society began to show support for LGBQ rights, it became less popular to be overtly homophobic.

Despite this, one recent reminder that heterosexism still exists was the Pulse nightclub shooting in Orlando in 2016. The LGBTQ nightclub was hosting "Latin Night," when Omar Mateen began open fire on the patrons inside. He killed 49 people (mostly Latinx) and injured 53 others. The massacre was the deadliest incidence of violence against LGBTQ people and the deadliest mass shooting by a single shooter in American history. Although the Federal Bureau of Investigation did not label the incident as a hate crime, the fact that Mateen targeted a gay nightclub both terrorized and traumatized the LGBTQ community, particularly LGBTQ people of color, who have historically viewed LGBTQ bars and nightclubs as their safe havens.

Systemic Heterosexism in Early U.S. History

Historical evidence supports the omnipresence of systemic heterosexism and violence throughout U.S. history. Since the English settlers arrived in the early 1600s, LGBQ people were arrested and imprisoned for *sodomy*, which was defined as oral sex, anal sex, or sex with an animal (Bronski, 2011). Although heterosexuals likely engaged in oral and anal sex, men who had sex with each other were the ones who were most arrested for or convicted of this crime. Through analyses of historical laws and legal documents from the 1600s through the 1800s, Crompton (1976) discovered that in the original colonies, sodomy was punishable by death and that an unknown number of men (and some women) had been executed over close to two centuries. From the 1800s to the mid-1900s, sodomy laws persisted throughout the United States, with many LGBQ people being arrested and convicted on such charges. However, by the end of this period, most states did not enforce harsher punishments; rather, arrestees usually just spent time in jail and paid various fines. It was not until 1961 that Illinois became the first state to remove sodomy laws from its criminal code, and by 1979, a total of 20 states had repealed their sodomy laws. By 2003, a total of 36 states had done the same—all after long legal battles from local to state to federal courts (Bronski, 2011). Later that year, through the SCOTUS ruling of *Lawrence v. Texas* (2003), sodomy laws that targeted LGBTQ people were deemed unconstitutional, and consensual same-sex sexual behaviors (that take place in the privacy of a person's home) were no longer viewed as criminal acts.

Because of sodomy laws, LGBQ people have historically had contentious relationships with police officers and the legal system. For instance, since the early 1900s, it was quite common for gay bars and businesses in New York City to be raided by police officers and for people to be arrested for either engaging in same-sex sexual acts (actual or perceived) or for dressing in gender nonconforming clothes. Police officers often raided these establishments, in attempts to bribe patrons who were afraid of being outed to their families and friends. On June 28, 1969, after one of many police raids of the Stonewall Inn in New York City, patrons fought back, and a revolt ensued. The Stonewall Uprising, often known informally as the Stonewall Riots, went on for the several days and gained media attention, eventually becoming known as the start of the national LGBTQ civil rights movement.

Systemic Heterosexism in the Contemporary United States

Besides the heterosexism of sodomy laws, systemic heterosexism has manifested in the United States in multiple ways. For example, when Title VII of the Civil Rights Act of 1964 was created to prohibit workplace discrimination based on sex, race, color, religion, and national origin, sexual orientation and gender identity were not included as protected classes (Berkley & Watt, 2006). Fifty years later, it is still legal in most states for LGBTQ people to be fired from their jobs for no reason other than their sexual orientation or gender identity. When states do not protect against employment discrimination or do not have clear language that lists sexual orientation and gender identity as protected classes, discrimination in this manner is completely legal.

Meanwhile, in states that do indeed have workplace protections in place for LGBTQ people, some people claim that forcing them to serve LGBTQ people is "against their religion" and that their religious rights are now being violated. Some small-business bakeries refused to make wedding cakes for same-sex couples, and wedding photographers refused to offer their services for same-sex couples, asserting that their religious freedom prevented them from doing so. Depending on the state in which this occurred, such behavior could be viewed as legal and justifiable or it could be considered discrimination and punishable by law. Some people might argue that same-sex couples should not force small businesses to be put into these types of situations and instead should find services elsewhere. Although this might seem like an easy solution, depending on where people live, there might not be many (or any) other viable options for these types of services. For instance, if only one professional photographer lives in a small town (or at least only one who is affordable) and that photographer refuses to take photos of a same sex wedding, the couple is experiencing differential treatment that a heterosexual couple would not have to worry about. In a similar way, if there was only one hospital in a small rural town and the hospital refused to serve LGBTQ people who urgently needed medical attention (because homosexuality went against the hospital's religious beliefs), they would be putting LGBTQ people's health at risk.

Perhaps the most well-known incident involving the idea of religious freedom as acceptable discrimination is the story of Kim Davis, a county clerk from Rowan County, Kentucky, who gained media attention after refusing to issue marriage licenses to same-sex couples. Shortly after the *Obergefell v. Hodges* (2015) SCOTUS decision, four same-sex couples went to their local courthouse hoping to legally wed; however, Davis declined to issue them marriage licenses, claiming she was acting "under God's authority." Even when ordered to perform her job duties, Davis refused; she was arrested and spent several days in jail. Although it is easy to chastise Kim Davis for her convictions, she was definitely not the only one who held such beliefs. Although the public opinion in support of same-sex marriage had shifted over time (i.e., from 35% in favor in 2001 to 55% in favor by July 2015), an estimated 39% of Americans opposed same-sex marriage around the time it was legalized (Pew Research Center, 2015). So, although more than half of the American population were celebrating the passing of this historic act, almost four out of 10 Americans were not. Perhaps this public opinion has changed since the law was set and enforced, as SCOTUS decisions eventually lead to changes in public opinion. For instance, after the historic *Loving v. Virginia* (1967) SCOTUS ruling (which put an end to all state bans on interracial marriage), public views of interracial marriage changed drastically.

Systemic heterosexism does not just emerge from the government or police but can also result from industries such as medicine and psychology. For instance, it was not until 1973 that "homosexuality" was removed from the *Diagnostic and Statistical Manual of Mental Disorders* and thus was no longer viewed as a diagnosable psychiatric disorder (Chernin & Johnson, 2003). Before this, psychiatrists, psychologists, and other practitioners considered LGBQ people (or those who engaged in same-sex sexual behavior) to be mentally unwell. For centuries, many people (e.g., doctors, therapists, religious leaders) attempted a number of sexual orientation change efforts (SOCEs). Also known as *reparative therapy* or *conversion therapy*, these SOCEs attempt to minimize a person's same-sex sexual desires and "transform" the individual into "being" heterosexual. Despite the many methods used (e.g., electroshock therapy, lobotomy, castration), research has found SOCEs to be ineffective and to have harmful long-term effects on the mental health of children and adolescents (American Psychological Association, 2009). Accordingly, the American Psychiatric Association, American Medical Association, American Psychological Association, and others have all denounced the use of SOCEs and view anyone who practices such therapies as violating ethical codes. In addition to ethical violations, SOCEs with minors younger than 18 years are now illegal in several states (e.g., California, New Jersey, Oregon, Illinois) and the District of Columbia because of the harm inflicted on children and because claims are not based on any empirical evidence and therefore are fraudulent (Bellware, 2015).

Systemic heterosexism against LGBQ people can also be illustrated through the ways that HIV/AIDS has been stigmatized and neglected in the United States. In the early 1980s, AIDS was initially labeled as the "gay disease" or "gay-related immunodeficiency disorder" because it was found mostly in gay men (Bronski, 2011). As a new disease, many of its causes and symptoms were unknown; yet, many Americans were quick to stigmatize gay men. Some public figures proclaimed that God was punishing gay men who contracted HIV; others stereotyped gay men as living with HIV or AIDS. Many gay men who were living with HIV/AIDS began to experience a dual discrimination in that they were rejected both for their gay identity and HIV status. In 1988, the National Gay and Lesbian Task Force reported more than 7,200 incidents of antigay harassment or victimization cases in the United States, with 17% being HIV/AIDS related (Berrill, 1992).

Perhaps one of the most blatant forms of heterosexist systemic discrimination was the way the U.S. government initially responded to HIV/AIDS. In 1982, just a year after the first cases were discovered, 422 AIDS-related deaths were reported across the United States; by 1990, the death count had increased to 31,000 (Hindus, 2006). Despite these alarming numbers, the U.S. government did very little to address the epidemic for the first 5 years. Despite having personal relationships with people who were living with the virus, as well as requests from scientists, physicians, and advocates, President Ronald Reagan was silent about the epidemic for 6 years. By the time he made his first speech on HIV/AIDS, 36,058 Americans had been diagnosed and 20,849 had died (Shilts, 1987). A month later, President Reagan issued an executive order and created the President's Commission on the HIV Epidemic. Many scholars viewed HIV/AIDS as a significant collective trauma for the LGBTQ community, given the high number of LGBTQ people who died in such a short period of time. To put this in context, the total number of HIV/AIDS-related deaths from 1981 to 1987 was 20,849—which means that about 9.5 people died per day for 6 years. During this time, about 7.5 times more people died of HIV/AIDS than from the attacks of September 11th (2,753 deaths) and 8.7 times more than at Pearl Harbor (2,403 deaths).

Similar to any other traumatic event, HIV/AIDS led to immense suffering for those who were affected directly and indirectly by the virus. While those who were living with HIV or AIDS suffered physically from bodily pain and psychologically from emotional anguish, those who witnessed their friends suffer and die also felt immense hurt and sorrow. In places such as New York City and San Francisco, many people (primarily LGBTQ people) suffered from bereavement overload—or the losses of multiple friends and lovers in such a short amount of time (Lehman & Russell, 1985). For example, in a qualitative study that documented the perspectives of gay men and lesbians who lost multiple friends to HIV/AIDS during the earlier years of the crisis, one participant revealed how he knew of 50 people who died of HIV/AIDS, that eight of those people were in his immediate support system, and that he lost seven of those people in the past 2.5 years (Biller, & Rice, 1990). To feel this much loss is very distressing, especially for people who witnessed their loved ones suffering from a disease that was so relentless and destructive. For LGBTQ people and others who never contracted the virus, watching friends agonize and in so much pain led many of them to suffer from survivor guilt—which parallels the feelings and symptoms of other types of trauma (Boykin, 1991). Finally, LGBTQ people who were shunned by their families and who inexplicably were able to "survive the plague" had to overcome the realities of HIV/AIDS, the trauma of multiple losses, the guilt of surviving, and the discrimination and bias associated with being LGBTQ.

A REVIEW OF THE SEXUAL ORIENTATION MICROAGGRESSIONS LITERATURE

Modeled after D. W. Sue et al.'s (2007) taxonomy, the taxonomy on micro-aggressions affecting LGBTQ people created by Nadal, Rivera, and Corpus (2010) includes a spectrum of themes, including the following:

1. *use of heterosexist terminology:* instances in which people use words or biased phrases or words that demean LGBQ people (e.g., someone saying "That's so gay!" to connote that something is bad or "No homo!" to emphasize that one is not LGBTQ);

2. *discomfort with/disapproval of the LGBQ experience:* instances in which someone conveys judgment or lack of support for one's sexual orientation identity (e.g., a coworker who is not interested in hearing about a female coworker's recent same-sex wedding, even though she consistently shows interest in heterosexual weddings);

3. *exoticization:* instances in which LGBQ people are tokenized, dehumanized, or objectified (e.g., a woman asks a new female coworker to be her "new lesbian best friend");

4. *assumption of universal LGBQ experience:* incidents in which heterosexuals assume that LGBQ people would fit some type of stereotype or would be similar to everyone in the same group (e.g., a gay man is asked for fashion advice, even though he has never expressed any interest in fashion and does not have a remarkable fashion sense); and

5. *assumption of sexual pathology/abnormality:* incidents in which an LGBQ person is presumed to sexually promiscuous, sexually deviant, or sexually predatory (e.g., a heterosexual man is intentionally distant and closed off toward his girlfriend's bisexual male friend who he biasedly believes will try to hit on him).

From 2010 until 2015, a total of 35 articles addressed microaggressions affecting LGBTQ people and communities, with most of the studies focusing specifically on sexual orientation microaggressions (Nadal, Whitman, Davis, Erazo, & Davidoff, 2016). Similar to the research on racial microaggressions, the studies show that LGBQ people are clearly able to identify and describe the types of microaggressions in their lives, as demonstrated by one study in which almost all of the participants reported experiencing interpersonal microaggressions (96%) and environmental microaggressions (98%), and a little more than one third of the sample (37%) reported blatant discrimination or victimization due to their sexual orientation (Woodford, Kulick, Sinco, & Hong, 2014). Further, another study revealed that an individual who has a strong sense of self and identity can securely cope with the microaggressions they are exposed to (Woodford, Paceley, Kulick, & Hong, 2015).

CASE STUDY

Carlos was a 24-year-old Mexican American man who was referred to therapy by Krystel, a case manager at the homeless shelter where Carlos was currently living. Other residents at the facility had been complaining to the staff that Carlos had been screaming in the middle of the night, which was affecting their ability to sleep. When Krystel met with Carlos, he informed her that he left his parents' home when he was 21 years old, after they discovered he was gay. He told her he had always had trouble sleeping because of intense nightmares and cold sweats in the middle of the night. In fact, he transferred to the current shelter 2 weeks ago because he had been kicked out of the last facility on the other side of town. Because of the shelter policies, Krystel was obligated to mandate that Carlos go to therapy in order to stay a resident; he hesitantly agreed.

Krystel referred Carlos to Dr. Jonathan Lozada, a local psychologist who offered low-fee therapy for residents of the homeless shelter on Saturday mornings. Dr. Lozada was a 42-year-old Latino American counseling psychologist (of Colombian and Peruvian descent) who had been practicing psychology for 12 years. He identified as an integrated therapist, which means he tends to utilize models and techniques from various theoretical orientations when he works with clients. During the week, he worked at a Veterans Hospital, where he ran an LGBTQ support group and a posttraumatic stress disorder support group. Krystel, who was familiar with Dr. Lozada's work, thought that he would be effective in providing therapy for Carlos.

When Carlos first met with Dr. Lozada, he immediately felt comfortable, as the therapist seemed warm, relatable, and compassionate. After Dr. Lozada described his approach to therapy, he invited Carlos to tell him about himself. Carlos revealed that he was 24 years old and had left his parents' home (where he had lived for all of his life) because his "crazy religious parents weren't exactly thrilled when they found out their oldest son was queer." Carlos immediately changed the subject and described how he had been living in and out of homeless shelters for the past 3 years. He reported initially staying with friends but overstaying his welcome with each of them. He then informed Dr. Lozada that to maintain his residence at the facility, he was required to attend these weekly counseling sessions.

When Dr. Lozada questioned Carlos about what he expected from therapy, Carlos replied that he "just wanted to be able to sleep again," revealing that he had nightmares nightly and woke up in the middle of the night or early morning screaming. He did not know when the nightmares started, but they had existed for as long as he could remember. When Dr. Lozada inquired about their content, Carlos stated he "never remembers the details" but that a nightmare usually involved him getting hunted, tortured, or killed by pretty much anyone—family members, strangers, priests, monsters, fictional characters, or animals. Dr. Lozada validated that the nightmares sounded frightening and assured Carlos that, in future sessions, he could bring up the nightmares whenever he liked.

At this point in the intake session, Dr. Lozada informed Carlos he had a list with a variety of questions aimed at getting a "full picture" of Carlos's life. After the therapist inquired about his family situation and childhood, Carlos disclosed that his parents were married (and had been since they were 19 years old) and had met in a small rural town in the Southwestern part of the United States, where they were both children of Mexican immigrant farmworkers. His father became a cab driver, and his mother worked at the local post office. Carlos reported having four younger siblings—Cedric, 21; Daniel, 18; Marta, 16; and Maribel, 13—all of whom were 3 years younger when he last saw them. Carlos claimed that he got along well with each of his siblings throughout his childhood and adolescence and that they all "looked up to him." He noted they got into many fights, as would be expected with five siblings and two parents living under the same roof in a three-bedroom house. Carlos admitted he was happy to have his own bedroom, since his brothers and sisters were close enough in age to share with a sibling of the same gender. Because of this, he felt good that he got at least a little privacy, as well as a little distance from the "crazy religious stuff" that was forced in all other rooms of the house.

As this was the second time that Carlos mentioned his "crazy" religious upbringing, Dr. Lozada gently interrupted him at this point, saying:

> So before we go any further, I noticed that this is your second time mentioning religion. I am wondering if you might be able to tell me a little bit more about what religion means or meant to you, especially since your family did not accept you when they found about you being queer?

Carlos shyly smiled and divulged that the pastors at his church would often preach about the "evils of homosexuality" and how "the gays" would all go to hell. Carlos revealed how it was hard to hear such messages at church growing up. When Dr. Lozada inquired further about how he dealt with these constant hateful messages, Carlos paused, looked up, and graciously replied, "Can we talk about that next time?" Dr. Lozada smiled, nodded, and moved on to the next set of questions.

When asked about his current living and work situations, Carlos replied that he had just moved into the shelter and liked it so far, despite knowing that others were complaining about his night terrors. Regarding work, Carlos explained that right before he left his parents' house, he was a student at a local community college, where he was taking a lot of general education classes. He grudgingly admitted he never finished his semester because it seemed "pointless" when he had nowhere to live. When asked about his career goals, Carlos reported receiving fairly good grades in high school and choosing to go to a community college to just "go with the flow" until he figured it out. Since then, he had found a lot of odd jobs, mostly in restaurants and in construction. He did not currently have a job, so he was volunteering his time doing chores at the shelter and helping with their children's program.

When asked, Carlos told Dr. Lozada that he did not do any drugs (although he had tried marijuana once) and that he only drank alcohol when it was offered to him. He asserted he "loves" being drunk because it helps him to sleep better; however, he also did not have the money to spend on alcohol every night, which was "probably the only reason why [he didn't] drink." Regarding his mood and current state, Carlos proclaimed he felt "fine" and had no intention of hurting himself or others. He also knew his "situation is depressing" but that he forced himself to "stop being sad" "a long time ago." Having finished the intake, Dr. Lozada shared that he uses a phase-oriented approach (Rosenberg, 2000) when working with gay trauma survivors and described the techniques that he could employ. Carlos said he would be open to trying this and that he would return next week.

In their second session, Carlos revealed more detailed aspects of his history. When asked about his sexual orientation, he said he had known he was attracted to boys ever since he was a young boy. In junior high, he felt especially conflicted because he could not stop thinking about boys or sex, which made him feel extremely guilty. He never told one person about what he was going through; instead, he tried his best to just "blend in." When Carlos started high school, he joined the church choir so he would be distracted. He reported that he enjoyed singing during the church services but found himself "zoning out" during the rest of the services—usually whenever the pastor preached hateful messages about gay people. He recalled times when the pastor made such declarations as, "Homosexuality was a moral decadence and sin," and "Gay people were enslaved by Satan." Carlos reported having visceral pains in his chest anytime he heard anything like this, saying that the messages felt as if they were literally stabbing him in the heart. Dr. Lozada queried him about how it felt to talk about all of these issues, and Carlos insisted that it "sounds sad" but he was "not sad about it anymore."

At the beginning of the third session, Dr. Lozada asked Carlos about his sleeping and his nightmares. After Carlos reported that the nightmares were still fairly frequent and that he could not remember them the next morning, Dr. Lozada recommended that he keep a dream journal (and pen) near his bed, so he could immediately jot down any or all content that he could remember, so that they could discuss the dream during their sessions. When Carlos displayed skepticism, Dr. Lozada provided some psychoeducation about the concept of dream analysis. He explained that some psychologists believe dreams are one way of interpreting people's unconscious, or unresolved issues they usually are not aware of. Although Carlos was still doubtful, he agreed to give it a try. It took him a short while to get used to the process; however, he followed the instructions and brought his dream journal to some of his therapy sessions.

For the next few sessions, Dr. Lozada and Carlos talked about his dreams. Dr. Lozada guided Carlos in thinking about how he was feeling throughout various parts of the dream, while asking him to examine whether any of the feelings in the dream resonated with current or past aspects of his life. Dr. Lozada also taught Carlos about a dream's manifest content (or the information in a dream that a person can recall in conscious or subconscious states) and latent content (or the hidden meaning of a dream that speaks to some unresolved issue in a person's unconscious). Carlos spoke about the major images that stood out most in his dreams (manifest content) and explored any potential meanings he could derive from them (latent content). Dr. Lozada was very helpful in guiding him in this process, to the point where Carlos was able to interpret many dreams on his own before even attending therapy.

In their seventh session, Dr. Lozada decided to finally inquire about the circumstances under which Carlos left his family's home. Before Carlos responded, he took a deep breath and sighed: "Okay, here we go." He discussed how he started searching for gay pornography on the Internet when he was 16 years old. He reported that he was initially shocked and embarrassed by what he found, but how eventually he really liked what he was discovering. He shyly shared how he began to masturbate while watching the pornography, which felt good physically but made him feel ashamed and guilty afterward. He reported engaging in this personal ritual throughout high school and up until he left home.

After being prompted to connect this story to his departure from home, Carlos stated he must have been at choir practice when he walked into the house and heard his parents yelling heatedly at each other. Not thinking anything of it, he went to his room and quickly shut the door behind him. When his parents realized that he was in the house, his father wrathfully yelled as he approached Carlos's room. As Carlos was about to open the door, his father barged in and pushed him against the wall, simultaneously crying and yelling, "*Estas maricon?*" (which translates to "Are you a faggot?" in English). Carlos's mother stormed in right behind him, also screaming and sobbing "Why would you do this to us? God is going to punish you! God is going to punish all of us!" Shocked and confused, Carlos remembered defensively replying, "What are you talking about?" He recalled his father storming out of the room crying, while his mother yelled, "Your sister found your videos on your computer!" He mentioned his mother sounding almost incomprehensible at this point, although, through her sobbing, he did hear messages such as "Why would you do this to us?" and "What did I do to raise you this way?"

Carlos maintained that the rest of the experience was "a blur." He vaguely remembered that his father stopped crying after about an hour but did not come out of his room for the rest of the night. Carlos had never seen his father cry in his entire life and reported feeling "very guilty" in being the one who "caused him" to enter that state. Carlos also loosely remembered his mother crying for what seemed like hours, and at some point she called their church pastor for help in finding an "exorcist." Carlos did not recall the exact details of that phone call, but he recalled feeling "terrified" because he had heard atrocious rumors about what his church had done to other gay kids. He could not remember any other details, but he did know that in the middle of the night, he packed a small backpack and left the house. He said he did not leave a note, nor did he say goodbye to anyone—not even to his younger siblings. After finishing this last sentence of his story, Carlos paused and detachedly stared into space for about 30 seconds. Dr. Lozada waited for a few more moments before gently questioning what he was thinking about. Carlos fleetingly replied with, "Oh, nothing. I just hadn't thought about that in a long time," abruptly returning to consciousness with, "What do you want to talk about now?"

CASE STUDY DISCUSSION AND
CLINICAL RECOMMENDATIONS

In examining Carlos's case, one might notice several concepts that have been discussed throughout the chapter (and throughout the book). First, it appears that Carlos might be reacting to several types of traumatic events, including the systemic and institutional trauma of heterosexism that he experienced through his church. To be a young person who is struggling with one's sexual identity and to hear so many negative, destructive messages about LGBTQ people can be quite damaging. Because of these messages, Carlos developed *internalized heterosexism* or *internalized homophobia* (Nadal & Mendoza, 2013), or the notion that being LGBQ is bad, immoral, or abnormal, and that heterosexuality is good, moral, and normal. Internalized heterosexism had affected Carlos in multiple ways, including his attempt to repress his attraction to boys, his extreme guilt after watching gay pornography, and his self-blame for "causing" his father to cry. Further, he developed a fragile sense of self in that he tried to "blend in" to avoid any attention on him, else people suspect he was queer. When it came to academic achievement, he learned to "go with the flow" instead of striving to achieve; perhaps he did not have career goals because he did not think he was capable or worthy.

A second event that might potentially be labeled as a trauma involves the night that Carlos was outed and decided to leave home. It appears that he was having a normal day, until he discovered that his parents found out about his sexual orientation. The act of being "outed" by someone else can be quite damaging in itself and has many similarities to other traumatic events: (a) it can happen suddenly without any warning or preparation; (b) the person who is outed may feel completely out of control; (c) the person who is outed may experience serious physical or practical consequences, such as violence, losing a job, or being ostracized from a family or community; and (d) the person who is outed may experience severe psychological distress. It appears that many of Carlos's traumatic symptoms were related to being outed. First, he had nightmares, which apparently had occurred before his involuntary coming out but which appeared to have been exacerbated since the event. His nightmares entailed very vivid and atrocious images and acts, in which he was tortured, hunted, or killed; he usually woke from these nightmares in a cold sweat without remembering the details of what had occurred. Second, Carlos appeared to be avoidant of both the event, as demonstrated by his evading the subject in his therapy sessions, and the emotions related to the event. Third, Carlos exhibited some signs of dissociation in that he tended to space out whenever he felt some sort of distress or a memory of a past trauma was triggered (e.g., zoning out during church services or after discussing traumatic events).

As a gay-affirmative integrated therapist, Dr. Lozada used a variety of techniques. First, because Carlos's main concern was his nightmares, Dr. Lozada taught him about dream analysis as a way of uncovering some of the hidden meaning of his dreams. A psychodynamic therapist might argue that Carlos repressed a lot of his negative emotions and that his nightmares were how these unresolved issues were communicated or released. Further, Dr. Lozada seemed to meet Carlos where he was emotionally, without pushing any conversations or confronting issues that Carlos was not ready to deal with, which may also be indicative of the therapist's use of motivational interviewing. Because Dr. Lozada was mindful of Carlos's traumatic history, he knew that it would be hard for Carlos to navigate topics related to the trauma and thus remained patient with his process. He also wanted to avoid any triggers or retraumatizing that Carlos may not be equipped to handle just yet.

Further, Dr. Lozada provided a lot of psychoeducation for Carlos, which was very helpful, as it appeared Carlos had minimal knowledge of the process of psychotherapy. Being able to teach clients about some of these concepts through more accessible language can help them be more invested in the process, instead of feeling like "damaged goods" that need to be "fixed." The sharing of information about dream analysis seemed helpful for Carlos, as it enabled him to understand that dreams are not just random and arbitrary but are worthy of exploration.

While still early in their therapeutic relationship, Dr. Lozada, as an integrated therapist, may want to explore many directions. For instance, given that Carlos seemed to be disconnected from his emotions (e.g., saying that parts of his life "sound" sad but that he "isn't sad"), it might be useful to integrate techniques from somatic experiencing—a therapy that guides clients to pay attention to their bodily sensations, which helps them to connect to their emotions and hopefully heal from trauma. Perhaps Carlos had shut down emotionally because it was the only way for him to survive on the streets, and although some time has passed since the incident, his body may still feel threatened or hypervigilant, disallowing him from feeling any emotional connection. Moreover, it may be helpful for Dr. Lozada to assist Carlos in unpacking his feelings about religion or spirituality. Although he clearly had a negative experience at his church, it may be useful for Carlos to explore what aspects of spirituality are important to him, if any at all, and whether such spiritual practices might be useful in his healing.

5

Gender Microaggressions and Trauma

Gender is a socially constructed concept in which people are classified on the basis of their birth sex, phenotype, and other characteristics. Globally, people have traditionally been categorized as men or women, with their traits being listed as masculine or feminine. Throughout the history of the United States (and in most parts of the world), men have more power and privilege than do women—resulting in sexism on systemic, institutional, and individual levels. This chapter reviews microaggressions based on gender, or subtle forms of sexism that are typically directed toward women (and usually cisgender women). The chapter reviews the current state of sexism in the United States and highlights how overt sexism has become legally and socially unacceptable, resulting in more covert manifestations of sexism and gender microaggressions.

http://dx.doi.org/10.1037/0000073-006
Microaggressions and Traumatic Stress: Theory, Research, and Clinical Treatment, by K. L. Nadal

FROM HILLARY CLINTON TO SONIA SOTOMAYOR: CONTEMPORARY SEXISM IN THE UNITED STATES

Over the past decade, a series of events have suggested that women's rights have improved in the United States. In 2008, when Hillary Clinton first ran for president, she became the first woman to ever win a primary election of a major party, which at the time was the closest a woman had ever been to being elected president. In 2009, she became the third woman to hold the position of U.S. secretary of state, and in 2016, she became the first woman to win the presidential nomination of a major party of the United States. In 2009, when Sonia Sotomayor was confirmed as a U.S. Supreme Court Justice, she became the first woman of color (and first Latina/o/x) to ever hold the position. In 2010, Elena Kagan's confirmation to the Supreme Court marked the first time that three women had ever served simultaneously on the highest court of the land.

Although these three successful women demonstrate the possible opportunities for power and success for women, they (and other women) have also experienced very public forms of sexism, which signify the current state of sexism in our country. For example, Hillary Clinton continually has been judged for her appearance, ranging from her outfits to her haircuts to how well people think she is (or is not) aging. Her leadership ability has often been compared with that of men; if she showed too much compassion, she was weak, yet if she showed too much sternness, then she was called any number of sexist labels. Other female political figures face this scrutiny too. When Michelle Obama became First Lady, the media also focused attention on her appearance. Major news programs covered when she got a new haircut, and others criticized her for wearing sleeveless dresses. Before their Supreme Court confirmations, Sonia Sotomayor was labeled as "sharp-tongued," "testy," and "nasty"; meanwhile, people questioned Elena Kagan's character because she had never been married or had children, deeming her "out of touch."

When men say they genuinely do not like a female politician's voting history or policies, they are certainly entitled to those opinions. Yet, when men say things such as, "It has nothing to do with her being a woman," they enact the same types of sentiment as described in colorblindness but instead with regard to gender. Many men believe they are fair and free from sexism; yet, in reality, they likely have implicit biases toward women, of which they are not even aware. Past researchers have referred to this phenomenon as *covert sexism* (Swim & Cohen, 1997) or *benevolent sexism* (Glick & Fiske, 2001). Covert sexism is less direct, less revealed, and often less conscious, in that many men believe themselves to be liberal but still view women as an inferior gender. For instance, most men believe in women's ability to enter any career field, yet they might still view female police officers as less strong, female physicians or scientists as less smart, and female politicians as having less effective leadership capabilities. A similar but nuanced concept is benevolent sexism or "a subjectively favorable, chivalrous ideology that offers protection and affection to women who embrace conventional roles" (Glick & Fiske, 2001, p. 109). So, when men believe it is their duty to protect and provide for women, they are indirectly saying women are helpless, need to be taken care of, or need a man to validate their existence.

Sexism can be seen in other career fields besides politics. For instance, studies have shown that women are heavily underrepresented in science, technology, engineering, and mathematics (STEM). One consistent finding is that women occupy only about one fourth of STEM careers, despite accounting for almost 50% of the U.S. workforce (Beede et al., 2011). One explanation for this disparity is that girls experience stereotypes from an early age that dissuade them from these fields; moreover, if girls do not see women in these STEM careers, the field would seem unrealistic (Shapiro & Williams, 2012). Women of color tend to be even more underrepresented in STEM fields, overcoming a double-bind of systemic racism and sexism that may also influence their beliefs in their capabilities or the general nurturing of their interests (Ong, Wright, Espinosa, & Orfield, 2011). A related trend has emerged in athletics, in that 14-year-old girls are 6 times more likely than their male counterparts to stop playing sports, even though girls and boys have similar levels of interest in sports from ages 6 to 9 years (Sabo & Veliz, 2008). Again, if girls are taught stereotypes that they are incapable of or unsuitable for something, it will likely affect their potential opportunities.

Finally, to understand gender microaggressions, another concept worth exploring is the idea of *rape culture*, defined as an environment in which (a) rape or sexual assault is prevalent, (b) the sexualization of women is normalized through the media or policies, and/or (c) violence toward women is excused or lacks repercussions (Ullman, 2010). Many scholars have discussed the ways in which American society in itself is a rape culture, in that women are highly sexualized and objectified yet are blamed or shamed when they are victimized by sexual assault (Nadal, Mazzula, & Rivera, 2017). Further because of policies and laws that do not protect women when they are sexually assaulted, sexual violence continues to perpetuate. As a result, women are taught to be hypervigilant, almost as if they should expect to be sexually assaulted, whereas minimal measures educate men to not be perpetrators.

A REVIEW OF THE GENDER MICROAGGRESSIONS LITERATURE

Although the study of sexism in its more covert forms has been ongoing for the past several decades (see Nadal, 2010, for a review), the study of sexism through the lens of microaggressions did not emerge until after D. W. Sue et al.'s (2007) article on racial microaggressions. In 2010, I proposed a taxonomy on gender microaggressions toward women (Nadal, 2010), which was confirmed in a qualitative study by Capodilupo et al. (2010). Through using interviews with women participants of diverse ages and racial backgrounds, the following themes emerged as some of the major types of microaggressions that women encounter in their lives:

1. *sexual objectification:* instances in which women are treated as sexual objects (e.g., a man stares at a woman's body or whistles at her and she walks by);

2. *assumptions of inferiority:* instances in which women are treated or perceived as intellectually or physically inferior (e.g., a male supervisor continually asks a male subordinate to complete major assignments but never asks a woman; a woman is presumed to not be strong enough to open a jar or carry a box);

3. *assumptions of traditional gender roles:* instances in which women are presumed to maintain stereotypical gender role norms (e.g., two female executives in a male-dominated office are tasked with planning the office party); and

4. *denial of the reality of sexism:* instances in which someone invalidates women's encounters with sexism (e.g., a man tells an acquaintance that she is "too sensitive").

Although the study of gender microaggressions has not flourished at the same speed as that of race or sexual orientation microaggressions, a few key studies are quite helpful in elucidating the nuances of gender microaggressions. First, Basford, Offermann, and Behrend (2014) used vignettes of gender microaggressions in fictional workplace settings to examine whether men and women could identify subtle discrimination equally; their findings indicated that although both men and women could label gender microaggressions as being discriminatory, women ranked those instances as being more severe. Thus, perhaps men can recognize when certain events are sexist; however, because they do not have the lived experiences of sexism, they might not realize how intense or traumatic those encounters can be. Second, Owen, Tao, and Rodolfa (2010) used the Microaggressions Against Women Scale to measure gender microaggressions in psychotherapy; their findings revealed that clients who perceived microaggressions in their psychotherapy sessions rated their working alliance and therapy outcomes lower. Accordingly, if microaggressions occur in therapy, they can affect the therapist–client relationship, which may also affect whether clients think therapy works at all.

One area of research regarding microaggressions and gender, still in its nascent stages but expected to grow, is intersectional microaggressions, particularly those related to race and gender. Lewis and Neville (2015) created the Gendered Racial Microaggressions Scale for Black Women and confirmed four types of microaggressions that Black women face: (a) Assumptions of Beauty and Sexual Objectification, (b) Being Silenced and Marginalized, (c) Strong Black Woman Stereotype, and (d) Angry Black Woman Stereotype. Aligned with this, Holder, Jackson, and Ponterotto (2015) found that Black women in corporate or executive positions reported feeling an array of workplace microaggressions, including being stereotyped, feeling invisible, or being excluded by their colleagues. Third, in a study exploring Latina/o Americans' experiences with microaggressions, Nadal, Mazzula, Rivera, & Fujii-Doe's (2014) findings indicated that Latina women reported more workplace microaggressions than did Latino men. Further, using a secondary qualitative analysis with six previous microaggression studies, Nadal, Wong, Sriken, Griffin, and Fujii-Doe (2015) revealed four types of microaggressions that women of color of various racial groups (e.g., Asian American, Latina, multiracial) experience: (a) women of color as sexual objects, (b) biased compliments on appearance, (c) Asian women as "damsels in distress," and (d) exclusion or isolation of multiracial women. It is clear that race influences microaggressions involving gender (and vice versa); thus, as mentioned earlier, intersectionalities must always be considered.

CASE STUDY

Marcia was a 47-year-old Asian American woman of Korean descent who had recently been named the first female executive vice president for a major Fortune 500 corporation in a major metropolitan city on the West Coast. Marcia was very proud of her new position, as she had worked really hard to get to where she was. As the child of immigrants and the oldest of three children, she felt a lot of pressure to do well in school and make her parents proud. She had worked in various positions in global marketing strategies and development, starting as a marketing representative right after she graduated from college 25 years ago. Marcia felt humbled and ecstatic to have made it to this position.

As the first woman in this leadership position, Marcia also felt awkward for being the only woman on the executive management team, and a woman of color at that. Yet, she also thought it was a great responsibility and that she could potentially advocate for other opportunities for women (especially women of color) in the company. Because of this, she felt pressured to do well, as she knew she was representing many others. In her first month, she went out of her way to stand out as a hardworking and exceptional employee. She set up personal coffee dates with her staff members and colleagues, she created programs to keep employees happy and productive, and she developed strong relationships with everyone in her department. Everyone was receptive, and Marcia was feeling very good about her new position.

After Marcia had been in the position for a few weeks, the CEO and other vice presidents invited her to what would be her first monthly meeting with the company's board of directors. At her previous job, Marcia had experience working with a board, so she did not initially feel too worried about this duty. However, this group was markedly different—all were men, most of whom were White and all of whom were significantly older than her. At her first meeting, a senior board member made a comment about how young Marcia was and teasingly asked to see her driver's license. At the same meeting, another board member told her that he did not see a ring and asked if she was dating anyone. Monthly, Marcia was subjected to these sorts of comments, some that seemed to be compliments (e.g., a board member who commented, "You look pretty today, Marcia"), and sometimes these statements seemed well-intended but degrading (e.g., one older board member said, "I like your dress," as he covertly glanced at her breasts). Marcia has become increasingly upset because she knows that none of the male vice presidents are ever "complimented" on their appearance. Despite this, she chooses not to do anything because she loves every other aspect of her job and figures that she can put up with a few sleazy men once a month.

After the end of a recent board meeting, one of the senior board members, Mr. Thomas, asked Marcia to meet him for a drink. She reluctantly agreed, thinking that she needed to remain on his good side. She asked him to meet her in the lobby bar of the hotel next to their building, so that she would be in a very public place and so could quickly leave right after she had one drink with him. Although their meeting began with a discussion of board-related issues, Mr. Thomas then asked Marcia if she had any interest in becoming the president of the company. She cautiously replied, "Of course, who doesn't want to be president of such a great company?" Mr. Thomas countered, "Well, I can make that happen," as he pulled a hotel keycard out of his blazer, and placed it on the table in front of her. With all of her might, Marcia (who was feeling disgusted and angry) smiled and calmly replied, "Well, Mr. Thomas, I do have to run to another meeting. It was very lovely meeting with you. I'll see you at the next meeting."

A month later, Marcia felt extreme anxiety and reluctance to go to work on the morning of the board meeting. She seriously contemplated calling in sick, but she knew that she had to face her fears and see Mr. Thomas. As she got up to enter the boardroom, her heart was palpitating so quickly that she felt her chest pounding. She took a few deep breaths and sat down at her usual seat. Mr. Thomas arrived shortly after and smugly smiled at her in a way that made her feel violated. For the rest of the meeting, she could not concentrate; she sensed he was peering at her, and she was too scared to look in his direction. When it was her turn to speak during the meeting, she stuttered, talked tangentially, and felt incredibly embarrassed that she was not doing a good job. After work, Marcia went home and immediately called her best friend, Frances, to tell her what happened. Frances suggested she file a sexual harassment lawsuit, but Marcia refused, saying it would be "career suicide." When Frances asked Marcia if she would consider going back to therapy, Marcia agreed, as she needed a place to vent and to feel support.

CASE DISCUSSION AND
CLINICAL RECOMMENDATIONS

Before exploring Marcia's case, it would be helpful to understand the legal criteria for sexual harassment. According to the U.S. Equal Employment Opportunity Commission (2016), sexual harassment involves "unwelcome sexual advances, requests for sexual favors, and other verbal or physical harassment of a sexual nature." Using this definition, it is clear that Mr. Thomas's actions could be grounds for filing a sexual harassment. Although not directly spoken, he implied that if Marcia went with him to his hotel room upstairs, he could help her push her career forward. Such behavior could be classified as an unwelcome sexual advance, although it potentially could become a "he said/she said" battle because there were no other witnesses.

It is unclear whether Marcia's experiences with gender microaggressions (e.g., male board members "complimenting" her on her appearance) could be legally classified as sexual harassment. Although she believed that each incident was sexist in nature (i.e., they did not comment on the men's appearance), there might not be enough "evidence" to classify the behavior as "harassment" or as being of a "sexual nature." They were not explicitly saying anything about her gender or about sex, but they did make her feel uncomfortable and extremely anxious. In this way, microaggressions can be more challenging because they are more difficult to prove than overt discrimination, often resulting in their continuance or even in an increase in their number or severity.

Despite Marcia's decision to not file a report or confront the behavior, the sexual harassment and the gender microaggressions affected many aspects of her life. First, it appears that some of her behaviors matched symptoms of traumatic stress: She had difficulty concentrating; she had the desire to avoid people and situations; and she had negative trauma-related emotions, such as feeling angry and violated. Second, the discrimination had affected her work performance. At her last meeting, she felt embarrassed after not performing as well as she should have. If she continued to perform in this way, she might feel even more distressed, which might exacerbate her symptoms. Further, this pressure might feel especially daunting given that she is the only female executive vice president and she feels that, whether she likes it or not, she is representing other women (and specifically women of color).

Marcia's situation demonstrates the catch-22 of responding to microaggressions or to any sort of discrimination, in which targets of discrimination weigh whether the confrontation is "worth it": If Marcia decided to file a complaint about Mr. Thomas or to confront the other male board members on their microaggressive behavior, she would face an array of potential consequences. Mr. Thomas and the other men might become defensive and tell her she is being oversensitive; they might preemptively tell others that Marcia is an "angry woman" or even an "angry Asian woman"—which might lead to stereotypes or perceptions of her work performance. If they were especially vindictive, they might deliberately go out of their way to damage her reputation or push her out of her position, citing her shaky work performance at the last meeting and other misconstrued examples to confirm her incompetence.

Because of these potential outcomes, Marcia passively chose to not confront the situation at all. She might have rationalized that she could live with the anxiety and the heart palpitations because she enjoyed the other aspects of her job. She may have also justified that because the harassment would only occur once a month, she could manage the situation. The idea that women expect or presume sexism (and objectification specifically) to be a normal part of life is one of the many dire consequences of systemic sexism. These feelings align with the tenets of objectification theory, which states that men are taught that women's bodies are objects they should have access to, whereas women learn to internalize being sexualized and treated as inferior beings (Fredrickson & Roberts, 1997). Further, Marcia's case also exemplifies that even when women become incredibly successful, they are still susceptible to sexual harassment and gender microaggressions. Despite the many laws that protect against sexual harassment in the United States, men's behaviors of sexualizing women are still normalized (and even encouraged), resulting in the continuation of various forms of sexism and hostile environments for women everywhere.

To effectively work with Marcia in treatment, one may consider an integrated approach using race-based trauma therapy (Bryant-Davis & Ocampo, 2006) and feminist therapy (Brown, 2008). With both therapies, the clinician can assist clients in recognizing that the trauma was based on systemic oppression (e.g., sexism, patriarchy, racism). The first few sessions could be spent allowing Marcia to share her experiences while assisting her in developing self-care strategies and navigating unsafe environments. Perhaps Marcia may feel unable to physically function at work because she feels unsafe and threatened; thus, therapy may focus on making choices in which she does feel safe and in control. As therapy progresses, it may be useful for Marcia to explore feelings related to the trauma, including feelings of self-blame (e.g., does she fault herself for agreeing to the meeting with the male board member?) and shame or shock (e.g., has she emotionally connected to what happened?). To connect with anger, the feminist therapist may facilitate experiential activities that allow Marcia to emote while also guiding her to identify coping skills and other techniques that assist in overcoming sexism. Throughout the therapy process, a feminist therapist may also inquire about how relational and power dynamics influence how Marcia participates in therapy, while encouraging self-advocacy skills too. In using both perspectives, it may be useful for the therapist to revisit whether Marcia would be interested in filing a sexual harassment lawsuit. Although such lawsuits are difficult to pursue in court, the belief and support of a therapist (especially as an affirmative authority figure) can be quite empowering for the client. In this way, the therapist can assist the client in navigating the legal system, specifically regarding the emotional distress that can emerge, reminding the client that she is not insane or paranoid, and that her trauma is real.

6

Gender Identity Microaggressions and Trauma

This chapter focuses on microaggressions based on gender identity, which is typically defined as an individual's personal sense of identification as male, female, transgender or gender nonconforming (TGNC), or some other description—regardless of the sex they were assigned at birth. Although the previous chapter primarily focused on experiences of cisgender women, this chapter examines gender through the lens of transgender people, genderqueer people, and people who identify along or beyond the gender spectrum. The chapter begins with the ways transgender people have been viewed in the United States and provides examples of how transgender bias manifests in the media. The growing literature on gender identity microaggressions is discussed, focusing primarily on microaggressions and TGNC people's experiences with trauma.

http://dx.doi.org/10.1037/0000073-007
Microaggressions and Traumatic Stress: Theory, Research, and Clinical Treatment, by K. L. Nadal
Copyright © 2018 by the American Psychological Association. All rights reserved.

FROM CAITLYN JENNER TO TRANSGENDER MURDERS: A SPECTRUM OF TRANSPHOBIA IN THE UNITED STATES

Although discrimination manifests in overt, systemic, and subtle ways for a number of historically marginalized groups, it is evident that violence and hate toward transgender people are still rampant. As previously mentioned, transgender people account for 10.5% of all hate crimes in the United States, despite being only 0.3% of the American population (National Coalition of Anti-Violence Programs, 2013). In 2016, there were 27 transgender murders—mostly targeting trans women of color (Ring, 2017)—the highest number since the number of hate crimes against transgender people first started being totaled in 1999. Further, over the past several years, incidences of transgender suicides have been much more visible in the media. For example, in December 2014, a 17-year-old transgender girl named Leelah Alcorn committed suicide after her parents forced her to go through conversion therapy. Her death was made public after she arranged for her suicide note to be posted on her Tumblr blog after she died. Following her death, lesbian, gay, bisexual, transgender, and queer (LGBTQ) leaders around the country advocated for Leelah's Law, forwarding a petition to put an end to conversion therapy for LGBTQ youth; President Obama supported the petition, and as mentioned in Chapter 4, bans on conversion therapy have already begun to be put in place in a few states across the country. Leelah's story matches previous research studies on transgender people and suicide showing that structural stigma (e.g., transphobic laws and policies) and internalized transphobia (i.e., the degree to which one has self-hatred about being transgender) were related to more suicide attempts (Perez-Brumer, Hatzenbuehler, Oldenburg, & Bockting, 2015). In other words, when trans people learn negative messages about their gender identities, and live in societies that normalize transphobia, they are more likely to attempt suicide. Relatedly, when transgender people are targeted for gender-based violence, they are also likely to commit or attempt suicide. In a study with 290 transgender people, almost half of the sample (44.8%) reported they had experienced in-school gender-based victimization and 28.5% reported a history of suicide attempt; further, the study revealed that people who were targeted for gender-based victimization were 4 times more likely to have attempted suicide than those who did not (Goldblum et al., 2012). Thus, it is crucial for society to create gender-affirming environments for trans people, not just so that they survive but also so they can thrive.

Despite these tragedies, some very positive gains have been made for transgender people in the United States in recent years. For instance, when *Orange is the New Black* (Kohan, Friedman, Hess, Hermann, & Tannenbaum, 2013–Present) was first released, the world was introduced to actress Laverne Cox, the first transgender person to play the role of a transgender character on a major television series. In 2014, Cox graced the cover of *Time* magazine (Steinmetz, 2014), discussing her perspectives about transgender visibility; in 2017, *Time* released an issue titled "Beyond 'He' or 'She'" (Steinmetz, 2017), which examined narratives of gender nonconforming people. In 2014, Janet Mock released her autobiographical book, *Redefining Realness: My Path to Womanhood, Identity, Love & So Much More*, in which she discussed her personal journey as a transgender woman of color; the book debuted on *The New York Times* bestsellers list. In May 2014, supermodel Geena Rocero came out in a Ted Talk that has now been viewed more than 3 million times. And in 2015, Caitlyn Jenner, a former U.S. Olympian, came out as transgender in an interview with Diane Sawyer (Sloan & Sawyer, 2015), later appeared in a photo shoot in *Vanity Fair* (Bissinger & Leibovitz, 2015), and also starred in a television series.

Although many other transgender people have been visible in the media, Caitlyn Jenner's story was popular for many reasons: (a) she has been a household name because she won the Olympic gold medal for the decathlon in 1976; (b) she was known as an athlete, which made people stereotype her male-presenting self as hypermasculine; and (c) most existing trans people in the media were not famous before they came out as trans, so many people were intrigued to see Caitlyn navigate a very public transition. Despite the general support from a lot of celebrities, politicians, and media figures, Caitlyn Jenner's coming out story also resulted in a lot of backlash. Many people refused to call her by her chosen name, with many people misgendering her by using male pronouns or the name she was assigned at birth. Others protested when she won the Arthur Ashe Courage award, stating that she had not done anything courageous of note. Further, within transgender communities and LGBTQ social circles, many people viewed Caitlyn Jenner's transition as one of privilege, as most transgender people have limited means and therefore are not able to transition as easily as she did. In fact, most transgender people, especially transgender women of color, are targeted by violence, harassment, poverty, or homelessness (see Nadal, 2013), none of which were part of Ms. Jenner's narrative.

Furthermore, as noted in previous chapters, discrimination toward transgender people has also taken more subtle forms. For example, in 2014, when Katie Couric asked model Carmen Carrera about her genitals in an interview, this was an inappropriate and invasive question that would likely never be asked a cisgender person. Similarly, in 2014, when former CNN personality Piers Morgan interviewed Janet Mock on his show, an onscreen description of Ms. Mock read "was a boy until age 18." Meanwhile, during the show, Morgan's Twitter account read, "How would you feel if you found out the woman you are dating was formerly a man?" Ms. Mock, along with many transgender supporters and cisgender allies, replied to Mr. Morgan via Twitter, calling him out on his bias. Instead of recognizing that he may have offended her and transgender people in general, Mr. Morgan reacted with Tweets such as, "Very disappointed in [Janet Mock's] tweets tonight. Deliberately, and falsely, fueling some sense of me being 'transphobic.' Unpleasant" and "As for all the enraged transgender supporters, look at how STUPID you're being. I'm on your side, you dimwits." So, although Mr. Morgan was likely not intentionally trying to be hurtful (in fact, he likely views himself as a transgender ally), his focus on Ms. Mock's birth sex and the sensationalizing of her transition are two common microaggressions that transgender people experience. Perhaps if he could fully empathize with transgender people and the dehumanization they undergo daily, he would not have been so defensive and might have been able to participate in a true teachable moment. Yet, as demonstrated throughout this book, people are often unable to admit to their biases because of their fear of being viewed as "bad" or prejudiced people.

A REVIEW OF THE GENDER IDENTITY MICROAGGRESSIONS LITERATURE

Nadal, Whitman, Davis, Erazo, and Davidoff (2016) conducted a comprehensive review of all the microaggressions publications that focused on LGBTQ people and found only five journal articles and dissertation studies that concentrated only on microaggressions toward transgender people. Although the research on gender identity microaggressions is scarce, the existing studies provide a solid foundation of the types of subtle forms of discrimination that transgender people face in contemporary times. For instance, Nadal, Rivera, and Corpus (2010) proposed a taxonomy of microaggressions that LGBTQ people in general face, and Nadal, Skolnik, and Wong (2012) conducted a qualitative study to confirm and add different types of microaggressions that transgender people encounter. These themes include the following:

1. *exoticization:* instances in which transgender people are objectified or tokenized (e.g., a person referring to someone as their "transgender friend"; a man who enjoys having sex with transgender women but refuses to date them);

2. *discomfort with/disapproval of the transgender experience:* instances in which people show condemnation or hostility toward transgender people (e.g., a media personality says that transgender people are pathological or confused; a person glares at a transgender person as she walks down the street);

3. *assumption of sexual pathology or abnormality:* instances in which transgender people are presumed to be sexually deviant or pathological (e.g., a cisgender man presumes that transgender women would be sexually promiscuous or kinky);

4. *denial of individual transphobia:* instances in which cisgender people deny their biases toward or about transgender people (e.g., a gay cisgender man says, "How can I be transphobic? I'm gay!"); and

5. *denial of bodily privacy:* instances in which cisgender people ask personal and invasive questions about transgender people's bodies (e.g., asking a transgender person if they have had "the surgery").

Nadal, Skolnik, and Wong (2012) also described anti-trans familial microaggressions (e.g., a parent who refuses to call a transgender person by their chosen name). Further, the researchers described four categories of systemic microaggressions toward transgender people: (a) lack of access to nonbinary public restrooms, (b) transphobic policies of the criminal justice system, (c) lack of competence in emergency health care, and (d) difficulty in changing government-issued identification that has incorrect gender markers. Although no known empirical research focuses on microaggressions and genderqueer or gender binary people, Nadal et al. (2016) proposed three categories of microaggressions experienced by genderqueer people:

1. *presumption of the gender binary:* instances in which people convey that it is only acceptable to identify as a man or a woman (e.g., a cisgender person asks a genderqueer person, "Why can't you just choose one? It would make your life easier!");
2. *incorrect gender pronouns:* instances in which someone uses a gender pronoun that does match the pronoun that a genderqueer person uses (e.g., a cisgender person refuses to call a genderqueer person "they" because they claim it is "incorrect grammar"); and
3. *misidentification:* instances in which genderqueer people are placed into categories they would not identify with, resulting in incorrect categorizing of genderqueer people (e.g., on a form, a social worker makes a presumption and labels a genderqueer person as a man).

Though this sampling of microaggressions toward genderqueer people is helpful, more studies need to include perspectives of TGNC people to fully understand the effects of microaggressions on traumatic stress and other psychological outcomes.

CASE STUDY

Keila was a 37-year-old heterosexual, Pacific Islander transgender woman (of Native Hawaiian and Samoan descent). She grew up in a very affirming family and community in Hawai'i, and her parents assisted her in her transition when she first came out to them as a 10-year-old girl. Because of this support, she felt confident to do anything. In high school, she was the star of the spring musical and vice president of her senior class. She was accepted into the prestigious local university, where she double majored in political science and Pacific Islander studies. After college, she worked as an aide for an elected official for a few years, and she was intrigued by the idea of running for office someday. She decided to apply to law school, so she spent a year studying for her LSAT exam and then applied to various schools around the country. When she was accepted into Ivy University (a pseudonym), one of the most prestigious law schools in the United States, she thought it would be a great opportunity to live and study on the mainland.

In addition to adjusting to the cold weather and the city life, then-26-year-old Keila experienced culture shock. Although she was accustomed to being around a mixed group of people in Hawai'i, she found herself not quite fitting in with the other students. No one seemed to know how to place her racially, some people presumed that she was Latina and spoke Spanish to her, and others asked about her ethnicity within a minute of meeting her. When she told classmates that she was Native Hawaiian and Samoan, people reacted in a spectrum of ways, from exoticizing comments to ignorant questions. Regarding her gender, no one really questioned her; because she passed, she did not feel the need to disclose. As weeks went by and she heard some peers disparage trans people in a class discussion about gender and law, she was glad she had not outed herself. She reminded herself that she was there primarily for an education, so she immersed herself in studying and tried not to think about her loneliness or homesickness.

Whenever Keila was bored or restless between study sessions, she video chatted with her friends and family back home, or communicated with them via social media. However, when she was feeling especially lonely, she visited transgender-specific dating websites that catered to men who were interested in transgender women. She liked the attention she received from the men on the site, and it seemed to be a harmless way to kill time between classes and studying. For the first year of law school, she chatted with a few men quite regularly and met some of them whenever she felt like leaving the house. She knew she was not interested in anything serious, so she dated around and had a few sexual encounters from time to time while she was finishing school.

Right before Keila graduated with her law degree, one of her professors invited her to stay local and work at her law firm while she studied for her bar exam. Keila had never really considered staying on the mainland; yet, because she knew that this was a superb career opportunity, she decided to take her professor up on her offer. She spent the year studying for her bar exam while working directly under the supervision of her former professor. Again, she did not have much of a social life, but she thought it was worth it for her career.

It was around this time that Keila (who was 30 years old) met Ian, a 32-year-old Puerto Rican cisgender man, through one of the online websites. Ian lived nearby and worked as an executive in a corporation downtown. After a series of flirty messages online, Ian asked Keila out to meet, and she agreed. On their first date, he wined and dined her, and she felt extremely validated by his kindness and flirtatiousness. That night, she went over to his condo and they had sex for the first time. She really liked Ian, and she told him that she wanted to see him again, and he enthusiastically agreed. When Keila passed her bar exam a month later, she called Ian and told him that she wanted to celebrate. Again, he took her out to dinner, and then to his apartment, where they had another passionate night together. Keila told Ian how she wanted to see him more often, and he said he wanted the same. For the next several months, they saw each other regularly and spent the night at each other's apartments.

As Keila's career started to take off, she found herself having to attend various social events around town, many of which were formal and to which colleagues brought partners or dates. She asked Ian, whom she presumed was her boyfriend, if he would like to attend an event with her. He politely declined, saying he had another event that evening. When another event came up a month later, she again asked him if he could join her, and he again turned her down, coming up with another excuse. Keila asked him if there was another woman, which he quickly denied. He shamefully told her that he really liked her and wanted to continue to see her but that he did not want their relationship to be public. Keila was crushed but pretended to be accepting. They continued to date each other for a year before she decided to break it off completely.

For the next 6 years, Keila had a series of these types of relationships with cisgender, heterosexual men with whom she had great sexual and romantic chemistry but who never wanted to be in an open, serious relationship with her. With each new relationship, she felt a glimmer of hope and thought that the man she was with would be the one who would be different from the prior ones. However, with each relationship, her heart was broken, and with each breakup, it became more difficult for her heart to heal. At 37 years old, Keila felt hopeless and worthless and blamed herself for not being able to hold onto a relationship. She believed that if she were cisgender, she would not have had this problem. She also imagined that if she were a little prettier, a little smarter, or a little bit more successful, then maybe one of the men would finally want to be out and proud in a relationship with her. When she noticed herself drinking a lot more than usual, and crying herself to sleep, she decided to seek therapy to help "clear her head."

CASE STUDY DISCUSSION AND CLINICAL RECOMMENDATIONS

Keila's story is one that might be viewed as an anomaly for transgender people in some ways, while being a very common story for trans people in other ways. For instance, as someone who was supported by her family, she was able to do well in school and eventually became a lawyer, which is an experience that is not common for trans people. Although Keila's is one of a few success stories (e.g., in 2010, the Honorable Victoria Kolakowski became the first openly transgender superior court judge in the United States), the majority of transgender people are not supported by their families, which often leads to the many disparities discussed throughout this book. Perhaps this case demonstrates that although a supportive family can be helpful in one's succeeding, systemic and interpersonal transphobia is so pervasive that even an accomplished person such as Keila is susceptible to discrimination, which may lead to mental health issues.

At the same time, Keila's case is common in that she is demonstrating the distress that transgender people frequently have when dating. Because transgender people are so stigmatized in the United States, many cisgender people who date, or are in romantic relationships with, transgender people experience stigma too. As a result, when they get into relationships with trans people, they may feel threatened or confused, and end up hurting the transgender person. Further, transgender people may need to navigate when to come out to people they are dating. If they come out to a potential partner too early, the act may come off as premature or presumptuous. If they come out to a potential partner too late, they may be accused of false advertising or lying. Fortunately, Keila did not have to endure this, as she purposefully met men on websites catering to transgender people. In this way, she was both smart and vigilant.

Keila also faced a common stressor that transgender people have with dating: that some cisgender men do not want to be in relationships with transgender women because they do not view them as "real" women or because they are afraid of the repercussions. In a study on microaggressions, one transgender woman said:

> [Men often tell me], "You're not girlfriend material. All I want from you is that sexual asset and that whole thrill of being with a transsexual and go on with my life and act like you never exist." Now, not only am I being objectified and sensationalized, I'm being less than human. (Nadal, Skolnik, et al., 2012, p. 66)

Being treated as an object or as less than human can be quite daunting when one is already struggling with many other acts of discrimination and bias in one's life. Experiencing a biased rejection from a romantic partner may be especially hurtful, especially when it happens often.

As did previous cases, this case demonstrates the ways in which intersectionalities may influence people's encounters with microaggressions. Although Keila's biggest stressors with microaggressions involved her dating life, she also recognized the subtle biases she has faced because of her race. Perhaps race also influences her dating experiences in ways that are not presented in the case (as likely do other factors, e.g., age, education, socioeconomic status). Further, because Pacific Islanders (and other indigenous peoples) have experienced genocide, have had their lands stolen, and have been erased from American narratives, it would be important to understand how historical trauma has also affected Keila as a Native Hawaiian/Samoan person. Perhaps her therapist can explore such topics with her, to not only gain new information but also guide Keila on how to use this information for her coping and insight.

Further, this case demonstrates that trauma does not always have to be conceptualized in the same way it is classified in the *Diagnostic and Statistical Manual of Mental Disorders* (5th ed.; *DSM–5*; American Psychiatric Association, 2013). Clearly, no life-threatening events were in this case, and Keila did not appear to experience any physical or bodily harm. Despite this, the constant discrimination she felt, from people she cared about, felt overwhelming and intense, which may have caused Keila significant distress. Based on the information given, it is likely that most psychologists and clinicians might not label Keila with any diagnoses related to trauma (and rather with a mood disorder, e.g., depression). Yet, it is important to consider that trauma-related disorders are the only diagnoses in the *DSM* that are said to be caused by an external event (i.e., trauma) and not by an individual's inability to cope or manage life stressors. In this case, Keila's dating problems may be primarily due to transphobia on systemic and interpersonal levels, something that is way beyond her control. Therefore, a therapist might reconsider pathologizing Keila's coping skills and criticize the oppressive environments instead.

Although feminist approaches (Brown, 2008) have been used with women and other marginalized groups, Richmond, Burnes, Singh, and Ferrara (2017) offered a feminist approach to trauma specifically for TGNC clients. First, to assess the client's experiences with trauma, it might be useful to administer a TGNC-specific measure, such as the Gender Minority Stress and Resilience Measure (Testa, Habarth, Peta, Balsam, & Bockting, 2015). Although such assessments were created for use in research, these surveys can be good starting points for an intake, particularly for understanding irrational thoughts and exposure to trauma. Second, it is necessary for the clinician to assert a TGNC-affirming stance—by overtly and genuinely describing one's commitment to TGNC people. Because TGNC people have been constantly pathologized or misdiagnosed, hearing such validations from a therapist can help to build rapport and trust. Similar to other feminist approaches, a TGNC-affirming feminist therapist would also provide psychoeducational techniques for self-advocacy, self-care, and developing a critical consciousness. In therapy, this can be done through the exploration of internalized transphobia or gender role socialization, cognitive restructuring, or by providing narratives of other TGNC people that validate a client's experiences and processes. If a therapist were to use these techniques with Keila, it is expected that she could feel validated—especially if she realized she was not alone in her experiences. She might be able to unpack some of the negative beliefs she has internalized about being transgender, which affect how she feels about her appearance or her abilities. While she may cognitively know that she is intelligent, kind, resilient, and attractive (and has the evidence to support this), she may still hold many insecurities that she does not allow herself to connect with. Thus, giving her the permission to be vulnerable could be one way she can heal. Finally, in developing a critical consciousness, she may feel empowered to advocate even more for social justice, which may assist in her career development and bolster her passion to thrive.

7

Conclusion and Future Directions

Throughout this book, I have provided many examples of how various forms of discrimination (e.g., systemic discrimination, overt discrimination and hate violence, microaggressions) influence mental health, and trauma specifically. I have examined various types of discrimination (e.g., racism, heterosexism, sexism, genderism), as well as trauma as it is defined by the *Diagnostic and Statistical Manual of Mental Disorders* (5th ed.; *DSM–5*; American Psychiatric Association, 2013) I also expand the definition of trauma, by exploring constructs such as insidious trauma, race-based trauma, historical trauma, collective trauma, transgenerational trauma, and vicarious trauma. It is unfortunate that because of constraints on book length, the book did not cover all of the people and communities negatively affected by microaggressions. Thus, I must emphasize the need for readers to consider other groups that may experience traumatic discrimination or microaggressive stress. For instance, Keller and Galgay (2010) described the spectrum of

http://dx.doi.org/10.1037/0000073-008
Microaggressions and Traumatic Stress: Theory, Research, and Clinical Treatment, by K. L. Nadal

microaggressions that people with disabilities encounter in their everyday lives, ranging from being infantilized to being presumed to have cognitive deficits. Nadal, Griffin, et al. (2012) revealed the religious microaggressions experienced by Muslim people, ranging from the stereotype of being a terrorist to the pathologizing of their religious practices. Microaggressions can affect many other groups on the basis of size, social class, age, multiracial identity, undocumented status, adoption history, mental health history, and the intersections of these characteristics or circumstances. When people who have been historically marginalized experience an accumulation of these microaggressions, they may develop any of the symptoms described with the previous groups. Despite these limitations, I hope that this book has provoked some thoughts on future directions for psychology, as well as new and different ways to serve historically underserved communities. To conclude, I present some recommendations for how to integrate the information in this book into various systems and practices.

RECOMMENDATIONS FOR PSYCHOLOGICAL PRACTICE

Throughout the text, I have provided many theoretical and empirical approaches to trauma, such as race-based trauma therapies, feminist therapies, and so on. Regardless of which approach or theoretical orientation a clinician uses, one of the main points I hope to have conveyed is the need to reconceptualize the definition of *trauma*. Although it is necessary for the *DSM–5* and the *International Classification of Diseases* (10th ed.; World Health Organization, 1992) to differentiate trauma from other disorders, expanding the definition to include some of these more insidious, microaggressive forms of trauma can be helpful in guiding the millions of people who encounter these experiences in their daily lives. If psychologists and other clinicians do not explicitly name racism, sexism, heterosexism, genderism, ableism, classism, and other forms of discrimination as traumatic sources or events, they are continuing to assign responsibility for the psychological symptoms to the targeted group, instead of blaming the source or perpetrator. As mentioned throughout the text, the responses of survivors of traditionally conceptualized catastrophic and life-threatening events are often validated as "normal" or expected. Meanwhile, when people suffer from oppression and develop psychological distress, they are often diagnosed with depression, anxiety, adjustment disorder, or other psychological disorders, which indirectly suggests that the individual was not strong enough to cope with these life experiences. It is my hope that psychologists and other clinicians will validate the responses of survivors of oppression as normal or expected in the same way they validate those of war veterans, survivors of 9/11 and the Boston Marathon bombing, and survivors of sexual assault.

Second, for naysayers who believe that oppression in and of itself is not "as traumatic" an event as a "life-threatening" event, I challenge them to consider how the lives of people who experience frequent and intense discrimination are threatened regularly—through the visceral emotional pain they feel, the physical health issues that are effected, and their willingness to persevere and navigate the world. Many of these people feel their lives are out of control (e.g., they live in poverty, they have no power over how people treat or stereotype them). Many feel helpless and defenseless, which in turn often results in feelings such as anger, guilt, sadness, or disbelief. Even if years have passed since they encountered these discriminatory events, such feelings are often triggered by new and present-day encounters with microaggressions or discrimination that remind them of the trauma they suffered in the past. These incidents can affect their ability to cope with life stressors, may negatively influence their self-esteem or mental health, and might even strain or damage their relationships with their loved ones—all of which are symptoms that are typically associated with trauma and posttraumatic stress disorder (PTSD).

Third, to be clear, I must reiterate that not every form of racism, sexism, heterosexism, or other forms of discrimination would classify as a trauma. Instead, I believe that clinicians should consider factors such as context, quantity, quality, and impact. If someone encountered a less intense microaggression just once or twice in their life, she or he may not be as affected as someone who encounters severe discrimination every day of their life. For example, if people live in an affirming community and have a validating support system (context) and they experience a microaggression once in a while (quantity) that seems well intentioned, harmless, or even outdated (quality), they might not have a debilitating reaction. In fact, some people may be able to find humor in the instance (impact) and move on with their lives, hence making the event feel non-traumatic. At the same time, someone who faces a singular (quantity) but intense or hostile (quality) microaggression, in an environment where they already feel marginalized (context), they may feel so overwhelmed or shocked that they develop traumatic symptoms (impact). Even though the event occurred only once, its quality, context, and impact suggest that the event was traumatic.

Throughout the book, I have provided examples for psychologists and other clinicians to consider, but the clinical decisions you arrive at—with clients whose stories are similar—will be your own. In the same way that I believe in encouraging psychologists and other licensed professionals to choose their modalities and theoretical orientations, I believe therapists have the right to use their own clinical judgment in working with clients. Along with this, I believe that it is crucial for them to take into account all of the information presented to them, primarily regarding multicultural-related issues, when making these decisions. I also believe that psychologists and other practitioners have an ethical responsibility to be culturally competent in working with people who are different from them, namely, people from historically marginalized groups. Hence, I hope that the points made throughout the book are considered in genuine ways, as a way of enhancing people's lives.

RECOMMENDATIONS FOR
EDUCATION AND TRAINING

I hope that this text has given educators, training directors, and anyone who works with students or young people takeaways that you will continue to consider and teach others. First, it is necessary to critically examine the specific ways that your institutions and workplaces are (or are not) addressing discrimination, as well as the psychological effects of insidious forms of oppression. Are policies in place for addressing racism, sexism, heterosexism, genderism, ableism, religious discrimination, or other types of oppression? Are specific policies regarding bullying, sexual harassment, racial harassment not only in place but also practiced and promoted? If these policies do not exist, perhaps it would be helpful to devise some ways to approach this advocacy that are practical and effective. If these policies do exist, it would be beneficial for people to contemplate their effectiveness or brainstorm on what else can be done.

One of the questions that many educators have asked me throughout the years is whether I believe in the idea of *trigger warnings*, or statements that notify people of potentially traumatic or distressing material that will be presented or discussed. In educational settings, the question is whether trigger warnings are necessary to include in course syllabi, to "warn" students of what will be discussed in class. Because of these trigger warnings, some students have asked (or informed) professors about their inability to attend or participate in class.

From my experience as an educator for more than 15 years, I do not believe that trigger warnings need to be explicitly stated at the beginning of class, at least not in the way it is typically framed. I do believe professors and other educators need to take care in how they teach about sensitive topics, particularly those related to oppression. In this way, I think that statements on the syllabus that discuss a professor's approach to multicultural issues, the nature of the course, and the course objectives, would help students know what to expect. At the same time, I believe it is necessary for students to learn and to grow from experiences that may sometimes be uncomfortable for them. As a result, I do not think students should be automatically excused from attending class without first having a conversation with their professor. For students who have suffered from severe forms of trauma and in whom conversations might trigger PTSD symptoms, a professor might decide that an excused absence is warranted. On the other hand, some professors might encourage these students to attend class (and to sit through it as much as possible) to guide them in working through their trauma. The professor could also encourage the student to work with the university counseling center, or some other clinical referral, so that they have a safe space to address these issues of trauma outside of class.

Relatedly, I do not agree with some authors who have stated that microaggressions lead college campuses to support a "victimhood culture"—or the notion that people who experience microaggressions have weaker coping skills or are hypersensitive. I also recognize that some people (often of historically marginalized groups themselves) deem others who react to certain microaggressions as "excessive," "oversensitive," or "dramatic." However, instead of pathologizing these individuals in this way, it would be beneficial to understand the person's past experiences with discrimination, which could provide a context for why their current reactions to discrimination may seem extreme. As mentioned throughout the book, I believe that strong reactions to microaggressions in the moment are often triggered by past traumatic discrimination and thereby would be retraumatizations. Hence, it would be crucial for educators and others to avoid criticizing or invalidating their students' reactions to microaggressions. Instead, educators might encourage students to seek treatment to address these traumas, provide referrals to culturally competent psychotherapists, and validate their reactions to their traumas as normal and expected.

Finally, to combat microaggressions (and the subsequent trauma), professors may consider ways that they can become scholar–activists by providing educational resources beyond the academy (e.g., sharing their work through public and accessible media, reducing academic jargon in their writing, participating in community organizations). Although it is understood that publishing in peer-reviewed journals is necessary for professional survival, sharing one's expertise with the general community can assist in teaching others about social justice. Facts, theories, logic, and science must be user friendly—especially if we want others to understand the basic elements of social justice. Education cannot be reserved only for those with privilege.

RECOMMENDATIONS FOR EVERYDAY LIFE

This last section focuses on suggestions for how to address overt discrimination, microaggressions, and the subsequent trauma that occurs, toward family members, friends, and other loved ones. First, it would be beneficial to validate that microaggressions and other forms of discrimination are real and affect various aspects of people's lives. Given that numerous studies have supported the existence and impact of microaggressions (see Nadal, Whitman, Davis, Erazo, & Davidoff, 2016; and Wong, Derthick, David, Saw, & Okazaki, 2014, for reviews), it might be necessary to use psychoeducational techniques to validate people's experiences, so that they know they are not alone and that their reactions are valid. As an example, when a client describes an instance with discrimination that left them feeling confused, a therapist can educate that client about the term *microaggressions* and the studies and literature that support their existence. Second, it is necessary to destigmatize mental health and mental health treatment, especially for marginalized communities that historically have had negative experiences with the mental health system, as well as those that encounter multiple mental health disparities that often go untreated. When friends, family members, or coworkers face any sort of oppression, it can be useful to ask specifically about potential traumatic stressors or other psychological effects. In doing so, you can assess whether your loved one needs any additional support, and if so, you can help them to get it.

Finally, for social justice advocates who combat systemic oppression, one necessary strategy is to engage in self-care—or activities and practices that assist in mindfully managing one's wellness and mental health. Self-care can include meditation, yoga, exercising, art, writing, psychotherapy, acupuncture, massage, and many other practices. For these advocates to continue their fights for social justice, they must engage in self-care and avoid burnout (Nadal, 2017). When social justice activists and community leaders can model healthy behaviors, they not only prevent microaggressive trauma in their own lives but also can be viewed as genuine, legitimate, and inspirational people who practice what they preach.

A FINAL MESSAGE TO SURVIVORS OF TRAUMA

Finally, I conclude this text by addressing anyone who has ever suffered from microaggressions or other discrimination in their lives—particularly those whose experiences were intensely stressful or traumatic. Although

I do not know the gravity of your struggles or the specifics of your situations, I do know that it is arduous work to overcome something that feels out of your control, specifically when regarding an identity that is important to you. Because of this, I want to remind you that you are not alone and to let you know that there are ways for you to heal. Trying to hold in or block memories of or feelings about these traumatic events might feel intuitive in order to escape your feelings of hurt, anger, or sadness. However, when we repress our emotions, or do not address our pain, these traumas have the potential to take control of other parts of our lives, including mental health, self-esteem, capacity to function, opportunities to succeed, and ability to maintain strong and healthy relationships.

If you need to talk about past traumatic experiences with microaggressions and discrimination, please find a loved one who can listen and validate your feelings and reactions. If you need professional help, please do not be ashamed to find it. Turn to your loved ones for support, and take advantage of any resources or social support you might have. Whatever you decide, please do not let the trauma win, because oppression is not your fault. Please know that your reactions to discrimination are normal and expected. Now is the time to heal.

References

Allport, G. W. (1954). *The nature of prejudice*. Garden City, NJ: Doubleday Anchor Books.

American Psychiatric Association. (2013). *Diagnostic and statistical manual of mental disorders* (5th ed.). Washington, DC: Author.

American Psychological Association. (2009). *Report of the American Psychological Association Task Force on Appropriate Therapeutic Responses to Sexual Orientation.* Retrieved from https://www.apa.org/pi/lgbt/resources/therapeutic-response.pdf

Americans With Disabilities Act of 1990, Pub. L. No. 101-336, § 2, 104 Stat. 328 (1991).

Balsam, K. F., Rothblum, E. D., & Beauchaine, T. P. (2005). Victimization over the life span: A comparison of lesbian, gay, bisexual, and heterosexual siblings. *Journal of Consulting and Clinical Psychology, 73*, 477–487. http://dx.doi.org/10.1037/0022-006X.73.3.477

Bandermann, K. M., & Szymanski, D. M. (2014). Exploring coping mediators between heterosexist oppression and posttraumatic stress symptoms among lesbian, gay, and bisexual persons. *Psychology of Sexual Orientation and Gender Diversity, 1*, 213–224. http://dx.doi.org/10.1037/sgd0000044

Basford, T., Offermann, L., & Behrend, T. (2014). Do you see what I see? Perceptions of gender microaggressions in the workplace. *Psychology of Women Quarterly, 38*, 340–349. http://dx.doi.org/10.1177/0361684313511420

Basile, K. C., Black, M. C., Breiding, M. J., Chen, J., Merrick, M. T., Smith, S. G., & Walters, M. L. (2011). *National Intimate Partner and Sexual Violence Survey: 2010 summary report*. Atlanta, GA: Centers for Disease Control and Prevention, National Center for Injury Prevention and Control, Division of Violence Prevention.

Bedard-Gilligan, M., Duax Jakob, J. M., Doane, L. S., Jaeger, J., Eftekhari, A., Feeny, N., & Zoellner, L. A. (2015). An investigation of depression, trauma history, and symptom severity in individuals enrolled in a treatment trial for chronic PTSD. *Journal of Clinical Psychology, 71,* 725–740. http://dx.doi.org/10.1002/jclp.22163

Beede, D., Julian, T., Langdon, D., McKittrick, G., Khan, B., & Doms, M. (2011). *Women in STEM: A gender gap to innovation.* Washington, DC: U.S. Department of Commerce.

Bellware, K. (2015, August). Illinois bans gay conversion therapy for LGBT youths. *The Huffington Post.* Retrieved from http://www.huffingtonpost.com/entry/illinois-bans-gay-conversion-therapy_us_55d668b4e4b020c386de2cc4

Berg, S. H. (2006). Everyday sexism and posttraumatic stress disorder in women: A correlational study. *Violence Against Women, 12,* 970–988. http://dx.doi.org/10.1177/1077801206293082

Berkley, R. A., & Watt, A. H. (2006). Impact of same-sex harassment and gender-role stereotypes on Title VII protection for gay, lesbian, and bisexual employees. *Employee Responsibilities and Rights Journal, 18,* 3–19. http://dx.doi.org/10.1007/s10672-005-9001-8

Berrill, K. T. (1992). Anti-gay violence and victimization in the United States: An overview. In G. M. Herek & K. T. Berrill (Eds.), *Hate crimes: Confronting violence against lesbians and gay men* (pp. 19–45). Newbury Park, CA: Sage.

Biller, R., & Rice, S. (1990). Experiencing multiple loss of persons with AIDS: Grief and bereavement issues. *Health & Social Work, 15,* 283–290. http://dx.doi.org/10.1093/hsw/15.4.283

Bissinger, B. (Writer), & Leibovitz, A. (Photographer). (2015, July). Caitlyn Jenner: The full story. *Vanity Fair.* Retrieved from http://www.vanityfair.com/hollywood/2015/06/caitlyn-jenner-bruce-cover-annie-leibovitz

Blume, A. W., Lovato, L. V., Thyken, B. N., & Denny, N. (2012). The relationship of microaggressions with alcohol use and anxiety among ethnic minority college students in a historically White institution. *Cultural Diversity and Ethnic Minority Psychology, 18,* 45–54. http://dx.doi.org/10.1037/a0025457

Boykin, F. F. (1991). The AIDS crisis and gay male survivor guilt. *Smith College Studies in Social Work, 61,* 247–259. http://dx.doi.org/10.1080/00377319109517367

Brave Heart, M. Y. H., & DeBruyn, L. M. (1998). The American Indian Holocaust: Healing historical unresolved grief. *American Indian and Alaska Native Mental Health Research, 8,* 56–78.

Braveman, P. A., Kumanyika, S., Fielding, J., Laveist, T., Borrell, L. N., Manderscheid, R., & Troutman, A. (2011). Health disparities and health equity: The issue is justice. *American Journal of Public Health, 101*(Suppl. 1), S149–S155. http://dx.doi.org/10.2105/AJPH.2010.300062

Breiding, M. J., Smith, S. G., Basile, K. C., Walters, M. L., Chen, J., & Merrick, M. T. (2014). Prevalence and characteristics of sexual violence, stalking, and intimate partner violence victimization: National intimate partner and sexual violence survey, United States, 2011. *Surveillance Summaries, 63*, 1–18.

Bronski, M. (2011). *A queer history of the United States.* Boston, MA: Beacon Press.

Brown, L. S. (2008). *Cultural competence in trauma therapy: Beyond the flashback.* http://dx.doi.org/10.1037/11752-000

Bryant-Davis, T. (2007). Healing requires recognition: The case for race-based traumatic stress. *The Counseling Psychologist, 35*, 135–143. http://dx.doi.org/10.1177/0011000006295152

Bryant-Davis, T., & Ocampo, C. (2005). Racist incident-based trauma. *The Counseling Psychologist, 33*, 479–500. http://dx.doi.org/10.1177/0011000005276465

Bryant-Davis, T., & Ocampo, C. (2006). A therapeutic approach to the treatment of racist-incident-based trauma. *Journal of Emotional Abuse, 6*, 1–22. http://dx.doi.org/10.1300/J135v06n04_01

Calmes, J., & Baker, P. (2012, May 9). Obama says same-sex marriage should be legal. *The New York Times.* Retrieved from http://www.nytimes.com/2012/05/10/us/politics/obama-says-same-sex-marriage-should-be-legal.html

Capodilupo, C., Nadal, K., Corman, L., Hamit, S., Lyons, O., & Weinberg, A. (2010). The manifestation of gender microaggressions. In D. W. Sue (Ed.), *Microaggressions and marginality: Manifestation, dynamics, and impact* (pp. 193–216). New York, NY: Wiley.

Carter, R. T. (2007). Racism and psychological and emotional injury: Recognizing and assessing race-based traumatic stress. *The Counseling Psychologist, 35*, 13–105. http://dx.doi.org/10.1177/0011000006292033

Carter, R. T., Mazzula, S. L., Victoria, R., Vazquez, R., Hall, S. S., Smith, S., & Williams, B. (2013). Initial development of the Race-Based Traumatic Stress Symptom Scale: Assessing the emotional impact of racism. *Psychological Trauma: Theory, Research, Practice, and Policy, 5*, 1–9. http://dx.doi.org/10.1037/a0025911

Carter, R. T., & Sant-Barket, S. M. (2015). Assessment of the impact of racial discrimination and racism: How to use the Race-Based Traumatic Stress Symptom Scale in practice. *Traumatology, 21*, 32–39. http://dx.doi.org/10.1037/trm0000018

Cartwright, B. Y., Washington, R. D., & McConnell, L. R. (2009). Examining racial microaggressions in rehabilitation counselor education. *Rehabilitation Education, 23*, 171–181. http://dx.doi.org/10.1891/088970109805029996

Chernin, J. N., & Johnson, M. R. (2003). *Affirmative psychotherapy and counseling for lesbians and gay men.* Thousand Oaks, CA: Sage.

Civil Rights Act of 1964, Pub. L. No. 88-352, 78 Stat. 241 (1964).

Comas-Díaz, L. (2016). Racial trauma recovery: A race-informed therapeutic approach to racial wounds. In A. N. Alvarez, C. T. H. Liang, & H. A. Neville (Eds.), *The cost of racism for people of color: Contextualizing experiences of discrimination* (pp. 249–272). http://dx.doi.org/10.1037/14852-012

Couric, K. (Interviewer). (2014, January 6). Carmen Carrera [TV episode]. *Katie Couric.* Retrieved from https://www.youtube.com/watch?v=u774QpimXS4

Crenshaw, K. (1989). Demarginalizing the intersection of race and sex: A Black feminist critique of antidiscrimination doctrine, feminist theory, and anti-racist politics. *University of Chicago Legal Forum, 1,* 139–167. Retrieved from http://chicagounbound.uchicago.edu/cgi/viewcontent.cgi?article=1052&context=uclf

Crenshaw, K., Gotanda, N., Peller, G., & Thomas, K. (Eds.). (1995). *Critical race theory: The key writings that formed the movement.* New York, NY: The New Press.

Crompton, L. (1976). Homosexuals and the death penalty in colonial America. *Journal of Homosexuality, 1,* 277–293. http://dx.doi.org/10.1300/J082v01n03_03

D'Augelli, A. R., Grossman, A. H., & Starks, M. T. (2006). Childhood gender atypicality, victimization, and PTSD among lesbian, gay, and bisexual youth. *Journal of Interpersonal Violence, 21,* 1462–1482. http://dx.doi.org/10.1177/0886260506293482

David, E. J. R. (Ed.). (2014). *Internalized oppression: The psychology of marginalized groups.* New York, NY: Springer.

Dawson, M. C., & Bobo, L. D. (2009). One year later and the myth of a post-racial society. *Du Bois Review, 6,* 247–249. http://dx.doi.org/10.1017/S1742058X09990282

de Mendelssohn, F. (2008). Transgenerational transmission of trauma: Guilt, shame, and the "heroic dilemma." *International Journal of Group Psychotherapy, 58,* 389–401. http://dx.doi.org/10.1521/ijgp.2008.58.3.389

DeCuir-Gunby, J. T. (2009). A review of the racial identity development of African American adolescents: The role of education. *Review of Educational Research, 79,* 103–124. http://dx.doi.org/10.3102/0034654308325897

DeJesus-Torres, M. (2000). Microaggressions in the criminal justice system at discretionary stages and its impact on Latino(a)/Hispanics. *The Justice Professional, 13,* 69–89. http://dx.doi.org/10.1080/1478601X.2000.9959574

Duckworth, M. P., & Follette, V. M. (Eds.). (2012). *Retraumatization: Assessment, treatment, and prevention.* New York, NY: Routledge.

Fairchild, K., & Rudman, L. A. (2008). Everyday stranger harassment and women's objectification. *Social Justice Research, 21,* 338–357. http://dx.doi.org/10.1007/s11211-008-0073-0

Feder, J., & Brougher, C. (2013). *Sexual orientation and gender identity discrimination in employment: A legal analysis of the Employment Non-Discrimination Act (ENDA).* Washington, DC: Congressional Research Service.

Federal Bureau of Investigation, Uniform Crime Reporting Program. (2014). *Hate crime statistics, 2013.* Washington, DC: Author. Retrieved from https://ucr.fbi.gov/hate-crime/2013

Ford, J. D., & Courtois, C. A. (Eds.). (2013). *Treating complex traumatic stress disorders in children and adolescents: Scientific foundations and therapeutic models.* New York, NY: Guilford Press.

Frantz, G. (2014). Individual and collective trauma. *Psychological Perspectives, 57,* 243–245.

Fredrickson, B. L., & Roberts, T. (1997). Objectification theory: Toward understanding women's lived experiences and mental health risks. *Psychology of Women Quarterly, 21,* 173–206. http://dx.doi.org/10.1111/j.1471-6402.1997.tb00108.x

Fredriksen-Goldsen, K. I., Simoni, J. M., Kim, H. J., Lehavot, K., Walters, K. L., Yang, J., ... Muraco, A. (2014). The health equity promotion model: Reconceptualization of lesbian, gay, bisexual, and transgender (LGBT) health disparities. *American Journal of Orthopsychiatry, 84,* 653–663. http://dx.doi.org/10.1037/ort0000030

Garcia, G. A., Johnston, M. P., Garibay, J. C., Herrera, F. A., & Giraldo, L. G. (2011). When Parties become racialized: Deconstructing racially themed parties. *Journal of Student Affairs Research and Practice, 48,* 5–21. http://dx.doi.org/10.2202/1949-6605.6194

Gates, G. J. (2011). *How many people are lesbian, gay, bisexual and transgender? Executive summary.* Los Angeles, CA: Williams Institute. Retrieved from http://williamsinstitute.law.ucla.edu/wp-content/uploads/Gates-How-Many-People- LGBT-Apr-2011.pdf

Glick, P., & Fiske, S. T. (2001). An ambivalent alliance: Hostile and benevolent sexism as complementary justifications for gender inequality. *American Psychologist, 56,* 109–118.

Goldblum, P., Testa, R. J., Pflum, S., Hendricks, M. L., Bradford, J., & Bongar, B. (2012). The relationship between gender-based victimization and suicide attempts in transgender people. *Professional Psychology: Research and Practice, 43,* 468–475. http://dx.doi.org/10.1037/a0029605

Harber, K. D., Podolski, P., & Williams, C. H. (2015). Emotional disclosure and victim blaming. *Emotion, 15,* 603–614. http://dx.doi.org/10.1037/emo0000056

Harrell, E. (2015). *Crime against persons with disabilities, 2009–2013—Statistical tables, Bureau of Justice Statistics.* Washington, DC: U.S. Department of Justice, Office of Justice Programs.

Hegewisch, A., Ellis, E., & Hartmann, H. (2015). *The gender wage gap: 2014. Earnings difference by race and ethnicity.* Washington, DC: Institute for Women's Policy Research. Retrieved from http://www.iwpr.org/publications/pubs/the-gender-wage-gap-2014-earnings-differences-by-race-and-ethnicity

Helms, J. E. (1995). An update of Helm's White and people of color racial identity models. In J. G. Ponterotto, J. M. Casas, L. A. Suzuki, & C. M. Alexander (Eds.), *Handbook of multicultural counseling* (pp. 181–198). Thousand Oaks, CA: Sage.

Helms, J. E., Nicolas, N., & Green, C. E. (2010). Racism and ethnoviolence as trauma: Enhancing professional training. *Traumatology, 16*, 53–62. http://dx.doi.org/10.1177/1534765610389595

Herek, G. M., & Berrill, K. T. (Eds.). (1992). *Hate crimes: Confronting violence against lesbians and gay men.* Newbury Park, CA: Sage.

Herek, G. M., Gillis, J. R., & Cogan, J. C. (1999). Psychological sequelae of hate-crime victimization among lesbian, gay, and bisexual adults. *Journal of Consulting and Clinical Psychology, 67*, 945–951. http://dx.doi.org/10.1037/0022-006X.67.6.945

Hinduja, S., & Patchin, J. W. (2010). Bullying, cyberbullying, and suicide. *Archives of Suicide Research, 14*, 206–221. http://dx.doi.org/10.1080/13811118.2010.494133

Hindus, L. A. (2006). Transparency in the age of AIDS: The reality and mythology of a disease. *Journal of Management Development, 25*, 996–1003. http://dx.doi.org/10.1108/02621710610708612

Holder, A. M. B., Jackson, M. A., & Ponterotto, J. G. (2015). Racial microaggression experiences and coping strategies of Black women in corporate leadership. *Qualitative Psychology, 2*, 164–180. http://dx.doi.org/10.1037/qup0000024

hooks, b. (2000). *Feminist theory: From margin to center.* London, England: Pluto Press.

Huynh, V. W. (2012). Ethnic microaggressions and the depressive and somatic symptoms of Latino and Asian American adolescents. *Journal of Youth and Adolescence, 41*, 831–846. http://dx.doi.org/10.1007/s10964-012-9756-9

Italie, L. (2017, February 7). Ghosting, shade, microaggression hit Merriam-Webster website. *Washington Times.* Retrieved from http://www.washingtontimes.com/news/2017/feb/7/ghosting-shade-microaggression-hit-merriam-webster/

Jagose, A. (1996). *Queer theory: An introduction.* New York, NY: New York University Press.

Jost, J. T., Rudman, L. A., Blair, I. V., Carney, D. R., Dasgupta, N., Glaser, J., & Hardin, C. D. (2009). The existence of implicit bias is beyond reasonable doubt: A refutation of ideological and methodological objections and executive summary of ten studies that no manager should ignore. *Research in Organizational Behavior, 29*, 39–69. http://dx.doi.org/10.1016/j.riob.2009.10.001

Kaiser, C. R., & Miller, C. T. (2003). Derogating the victim: The interpersonal consequences of blaming events on discrimination. *Group Processes & Intergroup Relations, 6*, 227–237. http://dx.doi.org/10.1177/13684302030063001

Keller, R. M., & Galgay, C. E. (2010). Microaggressive experiences of people with disabilities. In D. W. Sue (Ed.), *Microaggressions and marginality: Manifestation, dynamics, and impact* (pp. 241–268). New York, NY: Wiley.

Kellermann, N. P. (2001). Transmission of Holocaust trauma—An integrative view. *Psychiatry: Interpersonal and Biological Processes, 64*, 256–267. http://dx.doi.org/10.1521/psyc.64.3.256.18464

Kimerling, R., Weitlauf, J. C., Iverson, K. M., Karpenko, J. A., & Jain, S. (2013). Gender issues in PTSD. In M. J. Friedman, T. M. Keane, & P. A. Resick (Eds.), *Handbook of PTSD: Science and practice* (pp. 313–330). New York, NY: Guilford Press.

Kohan, J., Friedman, L., Hess, S., Hermann, T. (Executive Producers), & Tannenbaum, N. K. (Producer). (2013–Present). *Orange is the new Black* [Television series]. United States: Netflix.

Kosciw, J. G., Greytak, E. A., Palmer, N. A., & Boesen, M. J. (2014). *The 2013 National School Climate Survey: The experiences of lesbian, gay, bisexual, and transgender youth in our nation's schools.* New York, NY: GLSEN.

Kurashige, S. (2002). Detroit and the legacy of Vincent Chin. *Amerasia Journal, 28*, 51–55.

Lai, L., & Babcock, L. C. (2013). Asian Americans and workplace discrimination: The interplay between sex of evaluators and the perception of social skills. *Journal of Organizational Behavior, 34*, 310–326. http://dx.doi.org/10.1002/job.1799

Lawrence v. Texas, 539 U.S. 558 (2003). Retrieved from https://www.law.cornell.edu/supct/html/02-102.ZS.html

Lehman, V., & Russell, N. (1985). Psychological and social issues of AIDS. In V. Gong (Ed.), *Understanding AIDS* (pp. 177–182). New Brunswick, NJ: Rutgers University Press.

Lev-Wiesel, R. (2007). Intergenerational transmission of trauma across three generations: A preliminary study. *Qualitative Social Work: Research and Practice, 6*, 75–94. http://dx.doi.org/10.1177/1473325007074167

Lewis, J. A., & Neville, H. A. (2015). Construction and initial validation of the Gendered Racial Microaggressions Scale for Black women. *Journal of Counseling Psychology, 62*, 289–302. http://dx.doi.org/10.1037/cou0000062

Loo, C. M., Fairbank, J. A., Scurfield, R. M., Ruch, L. O., King, D. W., Adams, L. J., & Chemtob, C. M. (2001). Measuring exposure to racism: Development and validation of a Race-Related Stressor Scale (RRSS) for Asian American

Vietnam veterans. *Psychological Assessment, 13*, 503–520. http://dx.doi.org/10.1037/1040-3590.13.4.503

Lopez Levers, L. (2012). *Trauma counseling: Theories and interventions*. New York, NY: Springer.

Loving v. Virginia, 388 U.S. 1 (1967).

Luszczynska, A., Benight, C. C., & Cieslak, R. (2009). Self-efficacy and health-related outcomes of collective trauma: A systematic review. *European Psychologist, 14*, 51–62. http://dx.doi.org/10.1027/1016-9040.14.1.51

The Matthew Shepard and James Byrd Jr. Hate Crime Prevention Act of 2009, 18 U.S.C. § 249 (2009).

McCann, I. L., & Pearlman, L. A. (1990). Vicarious traumatization: A framework for understanding the psychological effects of working with victims. *Journal of Traumatic Stress, 3*, 131–149. http://dx.doi.org/10.1007/BF00975140

McKernan, S.-M., Ratcliffe, C., Steuerle, E., & Zhang, S. (2013). *Less than equal: Racial disparities in wealth accumulation*. Washington, DC: The Urban Institute.

Mejía, X. E. (2005). Gender matters: Working with adult male survivors of trauma. *Journal of Counseling & Development, 83*, 29–40. http://dx.doi.org/10.1002/j.1556-6678.2005.tb00577.x

Meyer, I. H. (1995). Minority stress and mental health in gay men. *Journal of Health and Social Behavior, 36*, 38–56. http://dx.doi.org/10.2307/2137286

Mitchell, G. (2008, December 16). Racial incidents and threats against Obama soar: Here is a chronicle. *The Huffington Post*. Retrieved from http://www.huffingtonpost.com/greg-mitchell/racial-incidents-and-thre_b_144061.html

Mock, J. (2014). *Redefining realness: My path to womanhood, identity, love and so much more*. New York, NY: Atria.

Mohatt, N. V., Thompson, A. B., Thai, N. D., & Tebes, J. K. (2014). Historical trauma as public narrative: A conceptual review of how history impacts present-day health. *Social Science & Medicine, 106*, 128–136. http://dx.doi.org/10.1016/j.socscimed.2014.01.043

Morgan, P. (Interviewer). (2014, February 5). Author Janet Mock joins Piers Morgan [TV episode]. *CNN*. Retrieved from https://www.youtube.com/watch?v=btmMVM23Ekk

Nadal, K. L. (2004). Pilipino American identity model. *Journal of Multicultural Counseling and Development, 32*, 45–61. http://dx.doi.org/10.1002/j.2161-1912.2004.tb00360.x

Nadal, K. L. (2010). Gender microaggressions and women: Implications for mental health. In M. A. Paludi (Ed.), *Feminism and women's rights worldwide: Vol. 2. Mental and physical health* (pp. 155–175). Santa Barbara, CA: Praeger.

Nadal, K. L. (2011). The Racial and Ethnic Microaggressions Scale (REMS): Construction, reliability, and validity. *Journal of Counseling Psychology, 58*, 470–480. http://dx.doi.org/10.1037/a0025193

Nadal, K. L. (2013). *That's so gay! Microaggressions and the lesbian, gay, bisexual, and transgender community.* http://dx.doi.org/10.1037/14093-000

Nadal, K. L. (2017). Let's get in formation: The role of psychology and social justice movements. *American Psychologist.*

Nadal, K. L., Davidoff, K. C., Davis, L. S., Wong, Y., Marshall, D., & McKenzie, V. (2015). A qualitative approach to intersectional and microaggressions: Understanding influences of race, ethnicity, gender, sexuality, and religion. *Qualitative Psychology, 2*, 147–163. http://dx.doi.org/10.1037/qup0000026

Nadal, K. L., Griffin, K. E., Hamit, S., Leon, J., Tobio, M., & Rivera, D. P. (2012). Subtle and overt forms of Islamophobia: Microaggressions toward Muslim Americans. *Journal of Muslim Mental Health, 6*, 16–37. http://dx.doi.org/10.3998/jmmh.10381607.0006.203

Nadal, K. L., Griffin, K. E., Wong, Y., Hamit, S., & Rasmus, M. (2014). The impact of racial microaggressions on mental health: Counseling implications for clients of color. *Journal of Counseling & Development, 92*, 57–66. http://dx.doi.org/10.1002/j.1556-6676.2014.00130.x

Nadal, K. L., Issa, M.-A., Griffin, K., Hamit, S., & Lyons, O. (2010). Religious microaggressions in the United States: Mental health implications for religious minority groups. In D. W. Sue (Ed.), *Microaggressions and Marginality: Manifestation, Dynamics, and Impact* (pp. 287–310). New York, NY: Wiley.

Nadal, K. L., Issa, M., Leon, J., Meterko, V., Wideman, M., & Wong, Y. (2011). Sexual orientation microaggressions: "Death by a thousand cuts" for lesbian, gay, and bisexual youth. *Journal of LGBTQ Youth, 8*, 234–259.

Nadal, K. L., Mazzula, S. L., & Rivera, D. P. (2017). *The Sage encyclopedia of psychology and gender.* Thousand Oaks, CA: Sage.

Nadal, K. L., Mazzula, S. L., Rivera, D. P., & Fujii-Doe, W. (2014). Microaggressions and Latina/o Americans: An analysis of nativity, gender, and ethnicity. *Journal of Latina/o Psychology, 2*, 67–78. http://dx.doi.org/10.1037/lat0000013

Nadal, K. L., & Mendoza, R. (2013). Internalized oppression and the lesbian, gay, bisexual, and transgender community. In E. J. R. David (Ed.), *Internalized oppression: The psychology of marginalized groups* (pp. 227–252). New York, NY: Springer.

Nadal, K. L., Rivera, D. P., & Corpus, M. J. (2010). Sexual orientation and transgender microaggressions in everyday life: Experiences of lesbians, gays, bisexuals, and transgender individuals. In D. W. Sue (Ed.), *Microaggressions and marginality: Manifestation, dynamics, and impact* (pp. 217–240). New York, NY: Wiley.

Nadal, K. L., Skolnik, A., & Wong, Y. (2012). Interpersonal and systemic microaggressions toward transgender people: Implications for counseling. *Journal of LGBTQ Issues in Counseling, 6,* 55–82. http://dx.doi.org/10.1080/15538605.2012.648583

Nadal, K. L., Vigilia Escobar, K. M., Prado, G. T., David, E. J. R., & Haynes, K. (2012). Racial microaggressions and the Filipino American experience: Recommendations for counseling and development. *Journal of Multicultural Counseling and Development, 40,* 156–173. http://dx.doi.org/10.1002/j.2161-1912.2012.00015.x

Nadal, K. L., Whitman, C. N., Davis, L. S., Erazo, T., & Davidoff, K. C. (2016). Microaggressions toward lesbian, gay, bisexual, transgender, queer, and genderqueer people: A review of the literature. *Journal of Sex Research, 53,* 488–508. http://dx.doi.org/10.1080/00224499.2016.1142495

Nadal, K. L., Wong, Y., Griffin, K. E., Davidoff, K., & Sriken, J. (2014). The adverse impact of racial microaggressions on college students' self-esteem. *Journal of College Student Development, 55,* 461–474. http://dx.doi.org/10.1353/csd.2014.0051

Nadal, K. L., Wong, Y., Griffin, K. E., Sriken, J., Vargas, V., Wideman, M., & Kolawole, A. (2011). Microaggressions and the multiracial experience. *International Journal of Humanities and Social Science, 1,* 36–44.

Nadal, K. L., Wong, Y., Sriken, J., Griffin, K., & Fujii-Doe, W. (2015). Racial microaggressions and Asian Americans: An exploratory study on within-group differences and mental health. *Asian American Journal of Psychology, 6,* 136–144. http://dx.doi.org/10.1037/a0038058

National Coalition of Anti-Violence Programs. (2013). *Lesbian, gay, bisexual, transgender, queer and HIV-affected hate crime violence in 2012.* Retrieved from https://avp.org/wp-content/uploads/2017/04/ncavp_2012_hvreport_final.pdf

National Institutes of Health. (2010). *Health disparities.* Washington, DC: Author. Retrieved from https://report.nih.gov/nihfactsheets/Pdfs/HealthDisparities (NIMHD).pdf

Neville, H. A., Gallardo, M. E., & Sue, D. W. (Eds.). (2016). *The myth of racial color blindness: Manifestations, dynamics, and impact.* http://dx.doi.org/10.1037/14754-000

Neville, H. A., Lilly, R. L., Duran, G., Lee, R., & Browne, L. (2000). Construction and initial validation of the Color Blind Racial Attitudes Scale (COBRAS). *Journal of Counseling Psychology, 47,* 59–70. http://dx.doi.org/10.1037/0022-0167.47.1.59

Noelle, M. (2002). The ripple effect on the Matthew Shepard murder: Impact on the assumptive worlds of members of the targeted group. *American Behavioral Scientist, 46*, 27–50. http://dx.doi.org/10.1177/0002764202046001004

Norris, F. H., Foster, J. D., & Weishaar, D. L. (2002). The epidemiology of sex differences in PTSD across developmental, societal, and research contexts. In R. Kimerling, P. Ouimette, & J. Wolfe (Eds.), *Gender and PTSD* (pp. 3–42). New York, NY: Guilford Press.

Obergefell v. Hodges, No. 14-556, slip op. at 22 (U.S. June 26, 2015). Retrieved from http://www.supremecourt.gov/opinions/14pdf/14-556_3204.pdf

O'Keefe, V. M., Wingate, L. R., Cole, A. B., Hollingsworth, D. W., & Tucker, R. P. (2015). Seemingly harmless racial communications are not so harmless: Racial microaggressions lead to suicidal ideation by way of depression symptoms. *Suicide and Life-Threatening Behavior, 45*, 567–576. http://dx.doi.org/10.1111/sltb.12150

Omni, M., & Winant, H. (2014). *Racial formation in the United States* (3rd ed.). New York, NY: Routledge.

Ong, M., Wright, C., Espinosa, L., & Orfield, G. (2011). Inside the double bind: A synthesis of empirical research on undergraduate and graduate women of color. *Harvard Educational Review, 81*, 172–209. http://dx.doi.org/10.17763/haer.81.2.t022245n7x4752v2

Owen, J., Tao, K., & Rodolfa, E. (2010). Microaggressions and women in short-term psychotherapy: Initial evidence. *The Counseling Psychologist, 38*, 923–946. http://dx.doi.org/10.1177/0011000010376093

Palmieri, P. A., & Fitzgerald, L. F. (2005). Confirmatory factor analysis of post-traumatic stress symptoms in sexually harassed women. *Journal of Traumatic Stress, 18*, 657–666. http://dx.doi.org/10.1002/jts.20074

Perez-Brumer, A., Hatzenbuehler, M. L., Oldenburg, C. E., & Bockting, W. (2015). Individual- and structural-level risk factors for suicide attempts among transgender adults. *Behavioral Medicine, 41*, 164–171. http://dx.doi.org/10.1080/08964289.2015.1028322

Peters, L., Slade, T., & Andrews, G. (1999). A comparison of ICD–10 and *DSM–IV* criteria for posttraumatic stress disorder. *Journal of Traumatic Stress, 12*, 335–343. http://dx.doi.org/10.1023/A:1024732727414

Pew Research Center. (2015). *Negative views of Supreme Court at record high, driven by Republican dissatisfaction.* Washington, DC: Author. Retrieved from http://www.people-press.org/files/2015/07/07-29-2015-Supreme-Court-release.pdf

Pierce, C., Carew, J., Pierce-Gonzalez, D., & Willis, D. (1978). An experiment in racism: TV commercials. In C. Pierce (Ed.), *Television and education* (pp. 62–88). Beverly Hills, CA: Sage.

Planty, M., Langton, L., Krebs, C., Berzofsky, M., & Smiley-McDonald, H. (2013). *Female victims of sexual violence, 1994–2010.* Washington, DC: U.S. Department of Justice, Office of Justice Programs, Bureau of Justice Statistics. Retrieved from https://www.bjs.gov/content/pub/pdf/fvsv9410.pdf

Plumm, K. M., Terrance, C. A., & Austin, A. (2014). Not all hate crimes are created equal: An examination of the roles of ambiguity and expectations in perceptions of hate crimes. *Current Psychology, 33,* 321–364. http://dx.doi.org/10.1007/s12144-014-9215-8

Pokhrel, P., & Herzog, T. A. (2014). Historical trauma and substance use among Native Hawaiian college students. *American Journal of Health Behavior, 38,* 420–429. http://dx.doi.org/10.5993/AJHB.38.3.11

Rice, E., Petering, R., Rhoades, H., Winetrobe, H., Goldbach, J., Plant, A., . . . Kordic, T. (2015). Cyberbullying perpetration and victimization among middle-school students. *American Journal of Public Health, 105,* e66–e72. http://dx.doi.org/10.2105/AJPH.2014.302393

Richmond, K., Burnes, T. R., Singh, A. A., & Ferrara, M. (2017). Assessment and treatment of trauma with TGNC clients: A feminist approach. In A. A. Singh & l. m. dickey (Eds.), *Affirmative counseling and psychological practice with transgender and gender nonconforming clients* (pp. 191–212). http://dx.doi.org/10.1037/14957-010

Ring, T. (2017, January 6). Virginia woman is 27th trans person murdered in 2016. *The Advocate.* Retrieved from http://www.advocate.com/transgender/2017/1/06/virginia-woman-27th-trans-person-murdered-2016

Rivera, D. P., Forquer, E. E., & Rangel, R. (2010). Microaggressions and the life experience of Latina/o Americans. In D. W. Sue (Ed.), *Microaggressions and marginality: Manifestation, dynamics, and impact* (pp. 59–84). New York, NY: Wiley.

Roberts, A. L., Austin, S. B., Corliss, H. L., Vandermorris, A. K., & Koenen, K. C. (2010). Pervasive trauma exposure among U.S. sexual orientation minority adults and risk of posttraumatic stress disorder. *American Journal of Public Health, 100,* 2433–2441. http://dx.doi.org/10.2105/AJPH.2009.168971

Rocero, G. (2014, March). *Why I must come out* [Video file]. Retrieved from https://www.ted.com/talks/geena_rocero_why_i_must_come_out

Root, M. P. (1992). Reconstructing the impact of trauma on personality. In L. S. Brown & M. Ballou (Eds.), *Personality and psychopathology: Feminist reappraisals* (pp. 229–265). New York, NY: Guilford Press.

Rosenberg, L. G. (2000). Phase-oriented psychotherapy for gay men recovering from trauma. In J. Cassese (Ed.), *Gay men and childhood sexual trauma: Integrating the shattered self* (pp. 37–73). http://dx.doi.org/10.1300/J041v12n01_03

Sabo, D., & Veliz, P. (2008). *Go out and play: Youth sports in America.* East Meadow, NY: Women's Sports Foundation.

Sachser, C., & Goldbeck, L. (2016). Consequences of the diagnostic criteria proposed for the *ICD–11* on the prevalence of PTSD in children and adolescents. *Journal of Traumatic Stress, 29,* 120–123. http://dx.doi.org/10.1002/jts.22080

Shapiro, J. R., & Williams, A. M. (2012). The role of stereotype threats in undermining girls' and women's performance and interest in STEM fields. *Sex Roles, 66,* 175–183. http://dx.doi.org/10.1007/s11199-011-0051-0

Sharby, N., Martire, K., & Iversen, M. D. (2015). Decreasing health disparities for people with disabilities through improved communication strategies and awareness. *International Journal of Environmental Research and Public Health, 12,* 3301–3316. http://dx.doi.org/10.3390/ijerph120303301

Shilts, R. (1987). *And the band played on: Politics, people and the AIDS epidemic.* London, England: Penguin.

Shipherd, J. C., Maguen, S., Skidmore, W. C., & Abramovitz, S. M. (2011). Potentially traumatic events in a transgender sample: Frequency and associated symptoms. *Traumatology, 17,* 56–67. http://dx.doi.org/10.1177/1534765610395614

Silver, R. C., Holman, E. A., Andersen, J. P., Poulin, M., McIntosh, D. N., & Gil-Rivas, V. (2013). Mental- and physical-health effects of acute exposure to media images of the September 11, 2001, attacks and the Iraq War. *Psychological Science, 24,* 1623–1634. http://dx.doi.org/10.1177/0956797612460406

Sloan, D. (Executive producer), & Sawyer, D. (Interviewer). (2015, April 24). Bruce Jenner—The interview [Television series episode]. In D. Sloan (Executive producer), *20/20.* Retrieved from http://abc.go.com/shows/2020/episode-guide/2015-04/24-bruce-jenner-the-interview

Solórzano, D., Ceja, M., & Yosso, T. (2000). Critical race theory, racial microaggressions, and campus racial climate: The experiences of African American college students. *The Journal of Negro Education, 69,* 60–73.

Steinmetz, K. (2014, May 29). Laverne Cox talks to *TIME* about the transgender movement. *Time.* Retrieved from http://time.com/132769/transgender-orange-is-the-new-black-laverne-cox-interview/

Steinmetz, K. (2017, May 29). Behind the covers story: Beyond "he" or "she." *Time.* Retrieved from http://time.com/4703058/time-cover-story-beyond-he-or-she/

Sue, D., Sue, D. W., Sue, D., & Sue, S. (2015). *Understanding abnormal behavior* (11th ed.). Belmont, CA: Wadsworth.

Sue, D. W. (2010a). *Microaggressions and marginality: Manifestation, dynamics, and impact.* New York, NY: Wiley.

Sue, D. W. (2010b). *Microaggressions in everyday life: Race, gender, and sexual orientation.* Hoboken, NJ: Wiley.

Sue, D. W., Bucceri, J. M., Lin, A. I., Nadal, K. L., & Torino, G. C. (2009). Racial microaggressions and the Asian American experience. *Asian American Journal of Psychology, S*(1), 88–101.

Sue, D. W., & Capodilupo, C. M. (2008). Racial, gender, and sexual orientation microaggressions: Implications for counseling and psychotherapy. In D. W. Sue & D. Sue (Eds.), *Counseling the culturally diverse: Theory and practice* (5th ed., pp. 105–130). Hoboken, NJ: Wiley.

Sue, D. W., Capodilupo, C. M., Torino, G. C., Bucceri, J. M., Holder, A. M., Nadal, K. L., & Esquilin, M. (2007). Racial microaggressions in everyday life: Implications for clinical practice. *American Psychologist, 62*, 271–286. http://dx.doi.org/10.1037/0003-066X.62.4.271

Sue, D. W., Lin, A. I., Torino, G. C., Capodilupo, C. M., & Rivera, D. P. (2009). Racial microaggressions and difficult dialogues on race in the classroom. *Cultural Diversity & Ethnic Minority Psychology, 15*, 183–190. http://dx.doi.org/10.1037/a0014191

Sue, D. W., Nadal, K. L., Capodilupo, C. M., Lin, A. I., Torino, G. C., & Rivera, D. P. (2008). Racial microaggressions against Black Americans: Implications for counseling. *Journal of Counseling & Development, 86*, 330–338. http://dx.doi.org/10.1002/j.1556-6678.2008.tb00517.x

Swim, J. K., & Cohen, L. L. (1997). Overt, covert, and subtle sexism: A comparison between the Attitude Toward Women and Modern Sexism scales. *Psychology of Women Quarterly, 21*, 17–34. http://dx.doi.org/10.1111/j.1471-6402.1997.tb00103.x

Szymanski, D. M., & Balsam, K. F. (2011). Insidious trauma: Examining the relationship between heterosexism and lesbians' PTSD symptoms. *Traumatology, 17*, 4–13. http://dx.doi.org/10.1177/1534765609358464

Tabaco, J. (2010). Pre and post trauma: Lessons from a Fil-Am Vietnam War veteran. In K. L. Nadal (Ed.), *Filipino American psychology: A collection of personal narratives* (pp. 243–250). Bloomington, IN: Author House.

Testa, R. J., Habarth, J., Peta, H., Balsam, K., & Bockting, W. (2015). The development of the Gender Minority Stress and Resilience measure. *Psychology of Sexual Orientation and Gender Diversity, 2*, 65–77. http://dx.doi.org/10.1037/sgd0000081

Thomas, K. R. (2008). Macrononsense in multiculturalism. *American Psychologist, 63*, 274–275. http://dx.doi.org/10.1037/0003-066X.63.4.274

Tolin, D. F., & Breslau, N. (2007). Sex differences in risk of PTSD. *PTSD Research Quarterly, 18*, 1–7.

Tolin, D. F., & Foa, E. B. (2006). Sex differences in trauma and posttraumatic stress disorder: A quantitative review of 25 years of research. *Psychological Bulletin, 132*, 959–992. http://dx.doi.org/10.1037/0033-2909.132.6.959

Torres, L., & Taknint, J. T. (2015). Ethnic microaggressions, traumatic stress symptoms, and Latino depression: A moderated mediational model. *Journal of Counseling Psychology, 62*, 393–401. http://dx.doi.org/10.1037/cou0000077

Truman, J. L., & Langton, L. (2014). *Criminal victimization, 2013*. Washington, DC: Bureau of Justice Statistics, Office of Justice Programs, U.S. Department of Justice.

Ullman, S. E. (2010). *Talking about sexual assault: Society's response to survivors.* http://dx.doi.org/10.1037/12083-000

United Nations Office on Drugs and Crime. (2012). *Global report on trafficking in persons 2012*. Vienna, Austria: Author. Retrieved from https://www.unodc.org/documents/data-and-analysis/glotip/Trafficking_in_Persons_2012_web.pdf

U.S. Census Bureau. (2010). *U.S. Bureau of the Census, age and sex composition: 2010 Census Briefs.* Washington, DC: U.S. Government Printing Office. Retrieved from http://www.census.gov/prod/cen2010/briefs/c2010br-03.pdf

U.S. Census Bureau. (2015). *U.S. Bureau of the Census, Population Estimates Program (PEP)*. Washington, DC: U.S. Government Printing Office.

U.S. Department of Labor, Bureau of Labor Statistics. (2014). *Persons with a disability: Labor force characteristics—2013* [Press release]. Washington, DC: Author. Retrieved from http://www.bls.gov/news.release/pdf/disabl.pdf

U.S. Department of Labor, Bureau of Labor Statistics. (2015). *Median usual weekly earnings of full-time wage and salary workers by selected characteristics, annual averages* [Press release]. Washington, DC: U.S. Government Printing Office. Retrieved from http://www.bls.gov/news.release/wkyeng.t07.htm

U.S. Equal Employment Opportunity Commission. (2016). *Facts about sexual harassment.* Retrieved from https://www.eeoc.gov/eeoc/publications/fs-sex.cfm

Wang, J., Leu, J., & Shoda, Y. (2011). When the seemingly innocuous "stings": Racial microaggressions and their emotional consequences. *Personality and Social Psychology Bulletin, 37*, 1666–1678. http://dx.doi.org/10.1177/0146167211416130

Watson, L. B., Marszalek, J. M., Dispenza, F., & Davids, C. M. (2015). Understanding the relationships among white and African American women's sexual objectification experiences, physical safety anxiety, and psychological distress. *Sex Roles, 72*, 91–104. http://dx.doi.org/10.1007/s11199-014-0444-y

Wong, G., Derthick, A. O., David, E. J. R., Saw, A., & Okazaki, S. (2014). The *what*, the *why*, and the *how*: A review of racial microaggressions research in psychology. *Race and Social Problems, 6*, 181–200. http://dx.doi.org/10.1007/s12552-013-9107-9

Woodford, M. R., Kulick, A., Sinco, B. R., & Hong, J. S. (2014). Contemporary heterosexism on campus and psychological distress among LGBQ students:

The mediating role of self-acceptance. *American Journal of Orthopsychiatry, 84,* 519–529. http://dx.doi.org/10.1037/ort0000015

Woodford, M. R., Paceley, M. S., Kulick, A., & Hong, J. S. (2015). The LGBQ social climate matters: Policies, protests, and placards and psychological well-being among LGBQ emerging adults. *Journal of Gay & Lesbian Social Services, 27,* 116–141. http://dx.doi.org/10.1080/10538720.2015.990334

Wooten, J. T. (1971, October 5). Compact set up for "post-racial" South. *The New York Times.* Retrieved from http://www.nytimes.com/1971/10/05/archives/compact-set-up-for-postracial-south.html

World Health Organization. (1992). *The ICD–10 classification of mental and behavioural disorders: Clinical descriptions and diagnostic guidelines.* Geneva, Switzerland: Author.

Yee, S. (2011). *Health and health care disparities among people with disabilities.* Berkeley, CA: Disability Rights Education & Defense Fund.

Zweigenhaft, R. L., & Domhoff, G. W. (2014). *The new CEOs: Women, African American, Latino, and Asian American leaders of Fortune 500 companies.* Lanham, MD: Rowman & Littlefield.

Index

About the Author

Kevin Leo Yabut Nadal, PhD, is a professor of psychology at both John Jay College of Criminal Justice and the Graduate Center (GC) at the City University of New York (CUNY). From 2014 through 2017, he was the executive director of the CLAGS: The Center for LGBTQ Studies at the Graduate Center (GC) at the City University of New York (CUNY), and he was the first person of color to hold this position in 25 years of the organization. From 2015 through 2017, he was the president of the Asian American Psychological Association (AAPA); he was the first openly gay person to serve in this role in the organization's 45-year history. Within AAPA, he cofounded the Division on Filipino Americans in 2010 and the Division on LGBTQ Issues in 2012. He is a National Trustee of the Filipino American National Historical Society (FANHS) and coordinated the FANHS national conference in New York in June 2016. He is also the cofounder of the LGBTQ Scholars of Color Network—a national network committed to academics and researchers who identify as LGBTQ people of color, which has been funded by the Annie E. Casey Foundation and the Arcus Foundation. For 7 years, he served as a training psychologist with the New York Police Department—advocating for mental health awareness toward citizens with a range of psychological disorders. He is the CEO of Nadal and Associates—his consulting firm which has allowed him to facilitate trainings and workshops with corporations, hospitals, and nonprofit organizations, as well as serve as an expert witness for various court cases.

Dr. Nadal received bachelor's degrees in psychology and political science from the University of California at Irvine, a master's degree in counseling from Michigan State University, and a PhD in counseling psychology from Teachers College, Columbia University. He is one of the leading researchers in understanding the impacts of microaggressions, or subtle forms of discrimination, on the mental and physical health of people of color; LGBTQ people; and other marginalized groups. He has published over 90 works on multicultural issues in the fields of psychology and education. He is the author (or coeditor) of numerous books, including *Filipino American Psychology: A Handbook of Theory, Research, and Clinical Practice* (2011); *Women and Mental Disorders* (2011); *That's So Gay: Microaggressions and the Lesbian, Gay, Bisexual, and Transgender Community* (2013); *Filipinos in New York City* (2015); and *The Sage Encyclopedia of Psychology and Gender* (2017).

In 2011, Dr. Nadal received the Early Career Award for Contributions to Excellence from AAPA. In 2012, he received the Emerging Professional Award for Research from the American Psychological Association Division 45: Society for the Psychological Study of Culture, Ethnicity, and Race. In 2015, he received the Outstanding Filipino Americans of New York award for Excellence in Education and Research. In 2016, he won the Faculty Scholarly Excellence Award at John Jay College of Criminal Justice. In 2017, he won the American Psychological Association Early Career Award for Distinguished Contributions to Psychology in the Public Interest.

For more information, visit http://www.kevinnadal.com or follow him on Twitter (@kevinnadal).